Legal Pluralism and *Shari'a* Law

Legal pluralism has often been associated with post-colonial legal developments especially where common law survived alongside tribal and customary laws. Focusing on *Shari'a*, this book examines the legal policies and experiences of various societies with different traditions of citizenship, secularism and common law. Where large diasporic communities of migrants develop, there will be some demand for the institutionalization of *Shari'a* at least in the resolution of domestic disputes. This book tests the limits of multiculturalism by exploring the issue that any recognition of cultural differences might imply similar recognition of legal differences. It also explores the debate about post-secular societies specifically to the presentation and justification of beliefs and institutions by both religious and secular citizens.

This book was published as a special issue of *Democracy and Security*.

Adam Possamai is Associate Professor in Sociology at the University of Western Sydney and is the current President of Research Committee 22 on the Sociology of Religion from the International Sociological Association.

James T. Richardson, J.D., PhD is the Foundation Professor of Sociology and Judicial Studies at the University of Nevada, Reno and the President Elect of the Society for the Scientific Study of Religions.

Bryan S. Turner is the Presidential Professor of Sociology and the Director of the Committee on Religion at the Graduate Center of the City University of New York, and concurrently the Director of the Centre on Religion and Society at the University of Western Sydney.

Legal Pluralism and *Shari'a* Law

Edited by
Adam Possamai, James T. Richardson and
Bryan S. Turner

Routledge
Taylor & Francis Group
LONDON AND NEW YORK

First published 2014
by Routledge
2 Park Square, Milton Park, Abingdon, Oxon, OX14 4RN

Simultaneously published in the USA and Canada
by Routledge
711 Third Avenue, New York, NY 10017

Routledge is an imprint of the Taylor & Francis Group, an informa business

This book is a reproduction of *Democracy and Security*, vol. 7, issue 4. The Publisher requests to those authors who may be citing this book to state, also, the bibliographical details of the special issue on which the book was based.

British Library Cataloguing in Publication Data
A catalogue record for this book is available from the British Library

ISBN 13: 978-0-415-82633-4

Typeset in Sabon
by Taylor & Francis Books

Publisher's Note
The publisher would like to make readers aware that the chapters in this book may be referred to as articles as they are identical to the articles published in the special issue. The publisher accepts responsibility for any inconsistencies that may have arisen in the course of preparing this volume for print.

Contents

Citation Information

The chapters in this book were originally published in *Democracy and Security*, volume 7, issue 4 (December 2011). When citing this material, please use the original page numbering for each article, as follows:

Chapter 1
Introduction
Bryan S. Turner, Adam Possamai, and James T. Richardson
Democracy and Security, volume 7, issue 4 (December 2011) pp. 311–316

Chapter 2
Legal Pluralism, State Sovereignty, and Citizenship
Bryan S. Turner
Democracy and Security, volume 7, issue 4 (December 2011) pp. 317–337

Chapter 3
Legal Pluralism, Family Personal Laws, and the Rejection of Shari'a in Australia: A Case of Multiple or Clashing Modernities?
Malcolm Voyce and Adam Possamai
Democracy and Security, volume 7, issue 4 (December 2011) pp. 338–353

Chapter 4
A Dual Legal System in Australia: The Formalization of Shari'a
Jan A. Ali
Democracy and Security, volume 7, issue 4 (December 2011) pp. 354–373

Chapter 5
More Than One Law for All: Legal Pluralism in Southeast Asia
Jamila Hussain
Democracy and Security, volume 7, issue 4 (December 2011) pp. 374–389

Chapter 6
The Social Construction of Legal Pluralism
James T. Richardson
Democracy and Security, volume 7, issue 4 (December 2011) pp. 390–405

Introduction

Bryan S. Turner,[1,2] Adam Possamai,[2] and James T. Richardson[3]

[1]Department of Sociology, The Graduate Center, City University of New York, New York, New York
[2]Centre for the Study of Contemporary Muslim Societies, University of Western Sydney, Australia
[3]Grant Sawyer Center for Justice Studies, University of Nevada, Reno, Nevada

Legal pluralism presents a complex theory of legal change, rendering any simple definition problematic. For the purposes of this introduction however, we may say that legal pluralism involves the presence of different legal traditions and institutions within a single political framework such as a state, thereby raising problems about how laws might be enforced and recognizing the prospect of contradictory traditions. The analysis of legal pluralism is often associated in modern legal theory with both the impact of globalization and with the cultural consequence of postmodernism. These two aspects are often combined into a single argument. It is argued that, with the rise of nation states through much of the nineteenth century, the sovereignty of states became a major issue leading to the development of modern taxation systems, a common language for the public domain, and the assertion of a single and integrated legal system. This rationalization of the law typically involved a critique of customary legal traditions. A unified sovereign state required a rational system of law based on the authority of secular courts with the backing of the state apparatus. With the growing intensity of globalization, it is now claimed that states have become more porous and more interconnected in global economic networks. The consequence is that states have to embrace legal pluralism arising from international laws on trade, labor laws, human rights legislation, and the workings of international courts such as the court of criminal justice and the European Court of Human Rights.

Postmodern jurisprudence has warmed to the idea of legal pluralism because it underpins the general postmodern argument that contemporary societies are becoming more complex and more fragmented. As a result the notion from the Enlightenment that law could provide a universal and timeless framework for the adjudication of disputes and general enforcement of social order has been seriously challenged by the complexity of late modern society. Postmodern philosophers have often found support from cultural anthropologists who have noted that in many colonial and postcolonial societies there are many forms of law surviving within a single polity such as aboriginal and Native American practices, customary laws, common law, and the laws arising from new constitutions.

In western societies, with migration and the creation of multicultural societies, there are now greater legal complexities in which, for example, there are demands for the practice of *Shari'a* courts at least in the case of domestic issues relating to marriage, divorce, and property settlements. The migration of Muslim communities into Europe has resulted in acrimonious public disputes about the role of Muslim tribunals in the United Kingdom, especially after the famous lecture of the Archbishop of Canterbury on the "inevitability" of the use of *Shari'a* in Britain in February 2008. Similar problems over the spread (real or otherwise) of *Shari'a* tribunals have arisen in Australia, Canada, and America. These tensions with Muslim religious practices have been exacerbated by the "war on terrorism" following the attack on the Twin Towers and the bombings in London and Madrid. While these attacks were the work of a small group of militants, the security threat has had a negative effect on the majority of law-abiding citizens.

These issues are now well known. However, these dramatic cases raise issues of a more implicit and complex nature relating to questions of individual freedom, liberty, and social complexity. It is in any case important not to rush to generalizations about the law in relation to religion and social complexity. The histories of colonization, migration, and modern multiculturalism are very different if we are comparing the United States, the United Kingdom, continental Europe, and so-called white settler societies such as Australia and New Zealand. It can be argued that legal pluralism has been more typical of British Commonwealth societies where customary laws and English common law found an accommodation. Singapore is one illustration of an ex-British colony that has *Shari'a*, English common law, and state legislation operating together in a relatively functional manner. Australia and New Zealand have both given some recognition to aboriginal customary laws, especially in tribal areas. And within the United States and Canada, some degree of recognition of tribal customs is granted by the State.

While American and Britain share aspects of a common law tradition, the Supreme Court in the United States plays a dominant role in the public domain and has jealously guarded its authority against alternative and competing traditions. In the recent debate about capital punishment in the United States, which is incompatible with American support for human rights conventions, Texas declared that it would never submit to "foreign" laws.

While the debate about legal pluralism has often been associated with the anthropology of law and with the study of postcolonial societies, the key issue in the current politics of multiculturalism is the question of religious freedom and secular laws. More specifically, the legal issue is whether liberal democratic societies can exercise tolerance with respect to Islam as we have seen in the debate about veiling. Can societies that have embraced the ideal of religious tolerance (mainly to bring an end to the wars between Catholics and Protestants) extend these liberal principles to Muslim communities?

The question of Islam and democracy has often focused on the question of veiling in public. France with its historical traditions of republicanism and *laïcité* has been the most decisive in its opposition to the veiling of women in public. While both America and Britain, with a tradition of religious tolerance going back to John Locke and to the establishment of puritan colonies in New England, have been less exercised by the question of the *berqa,* there is widespread unease about the possible spread of *Shari'a* values, courts, and judgements in secular societies.

This is the core of the contradiction that we attempt to address in this collection of articles. Can societies that are committed to liberal tolerance, cultural diversity, and recognition of multiculturalism exclude the *Shari'a* when orthodox Muslims claim they cannot live fully satisfactory lives of personal piety without access to the traditions of the *Shari'a*? If jurisprudential philosophers claim that contemporary societies are postmodern in their complexity, and that the unitary state and sovereign legal systems under the impact of globalization have given way to legal pluralism, what are we to make of attempts to marginalize or prohibit the *Shari'a*?

The United States rarely or never employs the discourse of "multiculturalism" in public debate. Because it has always been diverse, the use of the term appears to be superfluous. The actual word appears have been first used in Canada as a policy to address the threat of Quebec secession. In Australia it emerged with the decline of the "white Australia" policy that favored British and Irish immigration in order to create an environment that could cope with diversity from Italian, Greek, and East European migrants. In much of Europe, diversity arising from migration occurred much later and with more problems of assimilation and integration. Indeed at the beginning of 2011, the leaders of Britain, Germany, and France declared that multiculturalism had failed.

This U-turn in social policy is in part a response to the growth of right-wing parties that oppose migration and whose members are fearful of the cultural impact of Muslim immigration on national identity. Swiss cantons have prohibited the building of minarets, the Dutch Parliament is poised to pass a bill that will prohibit the traditional methods of slaughter by *halal* butchers demanding that the animals should be stunned before killing, the Danish public soured by the cartoon crisis have also turned against the openness that has been the basis of EU economic and social development, and the EU appears to be determined to keep the hurdle facing Turkish entry as high as possible. After the Archbishops's lecture, the British Labour government asserted that, while they could stomach "*Shari'a* compliant mortgages," they could not tolerate *Shari'a* playing a role in public affairs. These developments suggest that multicultural openness is being cut back, that there is a growing emphasis on legal and social uniformity rather than diversity, and that unrestrained migration is seen to be a threat to national character.

We could contend that two aspects of the rule of law are important. The first is that it should promote the principle of a level playing field—that is the law should not (and not be seen) to favor either majorities or minorities. In other words, this is a principle of fairness. Secondly (and this is closely related to fairness) the law should be consistent. One issue with the debate about *Shari'a* tribunals in Britain and elsewhere is that while Muslim tribunals were called into question, there has been no comparable discussion of the merits or otherwise of Jewish and Roman Catholic tribunals or other methods whereby religious groups settle internal disputes. One such example might be that the Amish community over the years has secured considerable legal advantages giving it immunity from interference from the state in some key areas such as education, but similar advantages have not been given to mosques. This silence appears to be unfair. There is also an element of inconsistency. *Shari'a* banking laws and what are referred to as *Shari'a* compliant mortgage arrangements are widespread in Europe and Australia—presumably because they generate income and provide services that are compatible with the financial framework of capitalism. However, other aspects of the *Shari'a* are not seen as suitable in the public domain.

Another inconsistency may be developing in the United States. In June 2011 New York State passed a law to recognize same-sex marriages. This law may raise problems of consistency in America because other states explicitly ban such marriages, with the result that couples in same-sex marriages may find that their marriages are simply not recognized elsewhere in the United States. There is another issue with such marriages, namely that they stretch the meaning of the concept of marriage to its limit. If states are willing to recognize same-sex marriage, why would they reject the practice of polygamy that is favored by some conservative Muslims? Furthermore, there has been a history of polygamy among fundamentalist Mormons, especially in western states such as Utah. Although polygamy has been officially banned in America, there is a practice within the fundamentalist Mormon group of plural marriage in which one man will (often clandestinely) set up a series of households with different women in order to practice informal polygamy.

To return to our opening comments about the alleged growth of legal pluralism with globalization and postmodernism, there appears to be much evidence to suggest in fact an opposite trend toward social and legal uniformity. Enthusiasm for cultural diversity appears to be waning in Europe as various right-wing or conservative parties in France, Denmark, and Finland have enjoyed some electoral success on a platform of limiting migration and containing the expression of Muslim practices and institutions in public. Opposition to the *berqa* has been followed by opposition to *Shari'a* tribunals. In Europe at least there appears to be a swing away from cultural diversity as an ideal. There is less evidence of such a transformation in Australia. However fears about "boat people"—the arrival of illegal immigrants in boats from Asia—have played a significant part in recent elections, and in general these illegal migrants are predominantly Muslim.

In many societies, therefore, the law appears to be used to constrain freedom of religion (at least in the public sphere) rather than enabling it under the banner of freedom of conscience. It is too soon to pronounce that these changes constitute a significant swing against liberalism and the open society, but there is little to suggest that negative media attention to Islam will decline as America now finds itself engaged in three wars with Muslim majority populations in Iraq, Afghanistan, and Libya. The prospects for religious tolerance in a global context look bleak.

In contrast to the idea of postmodern notions of fluidity, porous national boundaries, and floating personal identities, there appears to be substantial evidence that modern societies are being broken down into enclaves in which there is little reciprocity between migrant communities and host societies. The prospect of an "enclave society" is further cause to believe that we need to strengthen the bonds of common citizenship through social policies to rebuild a sense of community.[1] Campaigns in the United States by the Republican Party to severely limit immigration and the movement away from multiculturalism in Europe may be motivated by a sense that national unity is under threat, but the consequences of such developments is to further isolate and possibly to alienate migration communities.

To consider these diverse issues from both legal and sociological perspectives, this special issue includes five articles that explore legal pluralism in the West and in parts of Asia.

In "Legal Pluralism, State Sovereignty, and Citizenship," Bryan S. Turner argues that acceptance of religious law (of any variety) in the public domain can only work on the basis of strict secularization (the state's religious neutrality) and on the enforcement of gender equality. While the application of legal pluralism (and of a *Shari'a*-mindedness) does not have to be a threat to sovereign authority, Turner considers the problems posed by the possible development of a weaker state, the erosion of citizenship, and the growth of parallel communities.

Malcolm Voyce and Adam Possamai's "Legal Pluralism, Family Personal Laws, and the Rejection of *Shari'a* in Australia: A Case of Multiple or 'Clashing' Modernities?" explores in the Australian context the issues between *Shari'a* and family personal laws. Their paper applies S. N. Eisenstadt's theory of multiple modernities to understand legal pluralism, arguing that, to move the matter further, we should work toward a new multifaith pragmatic modern project.

Jan Ali's "A Dual Legal System in Australia: The Formalization of *Shari'a*" looks at the Muslim call for a dual legal system in Australia in relation to the establishment of *Shari'a* as a separate code of law and explores the basis upon which such a call rests. He concludes that in Australia, Muslims remain divided on ethnic and ideological grounds and that this community is fragmented. In the current situation, it would not only be premature, but also sociologically unsustainable, for this community to work and agree on a common set of Islamic legal codes.

Jamila Hussain's "More than One Law for All: Legal Pluralism in Southeast Asia" observes that in the neighboring countries of Australia, in Southeast Asia, *Shari'a* courts exist alongside civil courts. Focusing on Malaysia, Indonesia, and Thailand, Hussain argues that legal pluralism is not without its difficulties. In her exploration of these case studies, Malaysia appears to be at least one example where this system seems to work reasonably well.

James T. Richardson's "The Social Construction of Legal Pluralism" examines how the social construction of religious freedom and human civil rights can inform the current debate on legal pluralism. By covering variables such as different legal and judicial systems and the characteristics and the history of various societies, he creates a typology to analyze how *Shari'a* systems might develop and be allowed to flourish.

This special issue is the outcome of a conference on "*Shari'a* and Legal Pluralism" that was organized by the Centre for the Study of Contemporary Muslim Societies at the University of Western Sydney in Australia in July 2010. We are grateful for support from the University of Western Sydney for this conference and for the work being done at the Centre to address the pressing issues raised at the conference and in this special issue.

NOTE

1. Bryan S. Turner, "The Enclave Society: Towards a Sociology of Immobility," *European Journal of Social Theory* 10, no. 2 (2007): 287–303.

Legal Pluralism, State Sovereignty, and Citizenship

Bryan S. Turner

Department of Sociology, The Graduate Center, City University of New York, New York, New York
Centre for the Study of Contemporary Muslim Societies, University of Western Sydney, Australia

Early British colonialism was originally driven by the pragmatic trading needs of the East India Company, which only interfered with local custom and tradition in the interests of company profit. To some extent subsequent British governments adopted similar policies, and this strategy partly explains why postcolonial states such as Singapore, Malaysia, and most African states have always had legal pluralism. In many postcolonial societies in the late twentieth century, there was a political drive by indigenous peoples for customary law, and hence the principle of the unitary sovereign state was, at least in Latin America, weakened. In the contemporary situation, the prospect of accepting *Shari'a* in many European and North American societies has been rejected on precisely the issue of sovereignty, despite the fact that, for example, religious courts (both Jewish and Muslim) have often operated in such societies. The recent protest against the Archbishop of Canterbury's public lecture[1] is an obvious example. This article argues that acceptance of religious law (of any variety) in the public domain can only work on the basis of strict secularization (the state's religious neutrality) and on the enforcement of gender equality. However, if accepting religious law means in practice accepting third-party arbitration, then legal pluralism is not a direct threat to state sovereignty. In the United States, tribunals are not uncommon features of the legal system, and military tribunals have regularly been used to try enemy combatants. Furthermore, with the Internet some degree of informal but popular arbitration takes place between individuals in ways that are compatible with *Shari'a* as a consensus-seeking legal tradition. In a broader framework, however, the decline in direct personal taxation, the disappearance of conscription, and the growth of legal pluralism (within the framework of the nation-state) does imply both the development of a

An early version of this article first appeared in Bryan S. Turner, *Religion and Modern Society. Citizenship, Secularization and the State* (Cambridge: Cambridge University Press, 2011). It was also presented as a lecture to the Center for Middle Eastern Studies and the Center for European Studies at Harvard University. I am grateful to the discussion, which raised important questions about the original argument. The chapter has been much revised for this publication.

postnational and weaker state, as well as the erosion of citizenship. We need to be worried about both.

INTRODUCTION: THE ARGUMENT

Since 9/11 and similar terrorist events, the possibilities for pluralism and tolerance have been severely tested by a discourse of terrorism and state security. The development of an intelligent and cosmopolitan understanding between religious communities in Europe and America has been halted by a range of legal and political responses to "terrorism." In particular, Islam as a civilization has come to be defined as fundamentally incompatible with Western values. Muslim communities have thus been marginalized by a mixture of official processes of securitization and popular hostility. Early public criticism of veiling has been followed by mounting anxiety about the spread of *Shari'a* courts, and hence in this article I argue that legal pluralism in general and recognition of *Shari'a* courts in particular is an important if not critical test of the limits of multiculturalism.

In this discussion, I am less concerned with the nature of Islamic law and more interested in current arguments about its implementation and development in the West. In considering the *Shari'a* it is also at the outset worth distancing ourselves from classical Orientalist interpretations that have treated the *Shari'a* as a unified body of law that enjoined more or less undisputed authority and generality within traditional Muslim societies. The views of the great Orientalist Joseph Schacht, who wrote *Introduction to Islamic Law* (1964),[2] set the scene in 1935 by claiming that the "sacred law" of Islam was a comprehensive moral framework that regulated all aspects of the lives of Muslims. Although this interpretation of *Shari'a* has become the accepted view of many reformist movements in modern Islam, it was not the historical reality of Islam—as we can see from a brief commentary on law in the Ottoman Empire.

Shari'a has emerged as a more general political problem within Europe as a consequence of the expansion of the European Union. If *Shari'a* is a significant test of Western multiculturalism, then the prospect of Turkey joining the European Community is a significant test of European expansion and integration. The irony of Turkey's position in Europe is interesting, since Turkey is a clear-cut case of modern secularism at the constitutional level, but a profoundly Muslim society in terms of its civil society. The creation of the Turkish Republic involved the termination of the Caliphate, the suppression of *Shari'a* and traditional dress codes, and the adoption of French secularism to create a secular constitution. With the end of the Caliphate and the radical secularization of Turkish society, Islamic legal systems were often dislodged by Western positive law during colonization in the nineteenth and twentieth century. In the postcolonial period, there has been a significant revival of Islamic legal thinking in order to modernize legal practice and to make the impact of Islamic law more widespread in the community. This modernization of law often results in legal pluralism, as in for example Malaysia, where *Shari'a* competes with English common law, tribal codes, and human rights legislation.[3] In the Malay case Islamic legal practice has been modernized by lawyers who implicitly shared Max Weber's critique of the "irrationalities" of traditional Islamic legal practice.[4] And so *Shari'a* has been made more central in the public domain by lawyers who are more often than not trained in English legal practice, who wear pinstriped suits rather than customary garb, and whose mental attitudes and professional habitus are distinctively Western and secular. This development is not to say however that *Shari'a* has achieved a dominant or monopolistic position. Rather it is modernized and shares the legal stage with international law, human rights conventions, global corporate law, and an English common law tradition. In this context, how is the authority of religious law discovered and how is it implemented?

At the outset we need to recognize that there are long-standing problems in defining legal pluralism, but for the purposes of this article I shall simply describe it as a situation in which there are competing "bodies of law" within a given sovereign territory. It is often thought to be a problem emerging in the modern state, where the unified sovereignty of the state is challenged by different competing, and occasionally overlapping, systems of law. Although legal pluralism is often associated with both globalization and postcolonialism, in fact it had existed in Europe through the medieval period in terms of *ius commune*, commercial law (*lex mercatoria*), and ecclesiastical or canon law. Modern Muslims also like to imagine a time when the *Shari'a* had a dominant and exclusive authority, but this notion also turns out to be mythical.[5]

The debate about legal pluralism can be said to disguise a more urgent and deeper issue, namely the unity and sovereignty of the modern state. In this regard we can profitably open this discussion by quoting at some length from Peter Burns's *The Leiden Legacy*:[6]

> The conventional analyses of legal pluralism are unsatisfactory precisely because they take the myth of the polity as given. They accept the pretensions of the dominant nation state to absolute jurisdiction within its boundaries and attempt to rationalize the codes and customs of minorities within that framework. Generally they attempt to formulate the relationship in parallel with the model of "divided sovereignty," a fiction devised to rationalize the affiliation of autonomous states within a federal commonwealth.

Burns's critical assessment of the fiction of unified sovereignty helps us to frame the question regarding the possible introduction of *Shari'a* into modern secular legal frameworks. Following Burns, one might argue that it is not a threat to state sovereignty because legal pluralism is the norm rather than the exception: "legal pluralism is everywhere."[7] Brian Tamanaha approaches this issue from the standpoint of a pragmatist theory of law, which he claims embraces the postmodern criticism of universalism and essentialism without its "pessimism and sense of paralysis."[8] In fact most countries in which there is a Muslim majority are more accurately described as having a dual legal system in which the state and its laws are secular, but individual Muslims will bring family and financial disputes to *Shari'a* courts. In comparative terms, only Qatar strictly speaking has an official dual system where civil courts are completely independent of the *Shari'a* courts. Throughout much of the Middle East, all laws are claimed to have their source in the *Shari'a*. There is however significant variation in the treatment of Islamic communities and *Shari'a* in eastern Europe, Russia, and China, where "legal pluralism" is an appropriate label for societies that combine customary law, secular constitutions, and religious law.[9] In this article, I am primarily concerned with discussing the *Shari'a* in societies where Muslims are a minority and the state is emphatically secular. Although I come eventually to question the arguments of both Burns and Tamanaha, at this point we can simply note that any critical evaluation of *Shari'a* as a threat to the sovereignty of the secular state must take into account the historical evidence of legal pluralism.

While legal pluralism may have been common in earlier times, it has become increasingly an issue in the multicultural environment of modern states and is typically associated with postcolonial societies. For example, legal pluralism involving the recognition of customary, religious, and common law was a common arrangement in the British colonies, and hence it is still somewhat prevalent in Commonwealth countries. Although the argument is controversial, it can be claimed that early British colonialism was originally driven not by the ideology of a civilizational mission, but by the pragmatic trading needs of the East India Company, which only interfered with local custom and tradition in the interests of sustaining and protecting company profits. To some extent subsequent British governments adopted similar policies, and this pragmatic strategy partly explains why postcolonial societies such as Singapore, Malaysia, and most African states have always had legal pluralism. The policies of Dutch administration in former colonies in East Asia, most notably in Java, also recognized the importance of customary law, giving rise to complicated debates about the status of *adatrecht* in relation to *Shari'a*.[10] In many postcolonial societies, there was in the late twentieth century a political drive by indigenous peoples for the recognition of customary law and hence the principle of the unitary sovereign state was, at least in Latin America, weakened.[11]

With the contemporary "clash of civilizations," the prospect of accepting *Shari'a* in many European and North American societies has been rejected on precisely the issue of its threat to sovereignty. Critics tend to believe that religious arbitration (both Jewish and Muslim) provides a context for an underhand method of introducing *Shari'a* by stealth.[12] As we shall see shortly, the emergence of these forms of religious arbitration has raised a much more problematic issue, namely, what is law? Notwithstanding these technical issues around the legal character of tribunals and arbitration, the prospect of *Shari'a* courts operating in secular societies has given rise to acrimonious public debate. Recent protests against the Archbishop of Canterbury's public lecture on "Civil and Religious Law in England : A Religious Perspective," given on February 7, 2008 and the public dispute over the introduction of *Shari'a* into arbitration courts in Ontario, Canada are obvious contemporary examples.

This article argues that any acceptance of religious law (whether Jewish, Catholic, or Islamic) in the public domain can only take place on the basis of at least five important conditions: strict and visible secularization (the state's religious neutrality), the presence of one authority ("the law of the land") as the final supreme arbiter, the actual enforcement of gender equality, the defense of individual rights, and protection of common liberal values from legal judgements that represent minority traditions. Of course it turns out that satisfying these conditions is extremely difficult and much criticism of the idea of introducing the *Shari'a* has been precisely around the question of gender equality, liberal values, and individual rights.

The notion that there can be a final arbiter given the complexities of the modern world has been challenged, as we have seen, by authors such as Brian Tamanaha and Peter Burns. With globalization, it is often argued that the sovereignty of the state and its legal system has been compromised by the legal complexities of international relations, the rise of diverse commercial law systems, human rights legislation, and so forth. One standard criticism of legal pluralism is that it encourages various forms of "forum shopping" in which individuals or groups can exploit the differentiation and openness of the legal system to obtain judgements that are consistent with their own interests.[13]

However, Burns's argument, while persuasive, was developed to understand the role of law within the cultural, social, and religious diversity of the Indonesian archipelago. How far can we generalize from this Indonesian case study to conclude that state sovereignty is invariably a fiction and form some general view about the ubiquity of legal pluralism? Are all state fictions the same? It is worth dwelling on the Indonesian example because it well illustrates the complexity of legal pluralism and the tensions between customary, religious, and European courts. Various attempts at the beginning of the twentieth century to modernize the Indonesian legal system are illustrated by the publication of Cornelis van Vollenhoven's *Miskenningen van het adatrecht* in 1909.[14] This publication was an open juridical challenge to the conventional view that the Dutch state was the supreme master over the lands of the Netherlands East Indies. The *Miskenningen* exposed the bureaucratic muddle of decrees, statutes, ordinances, and regulations. Of course this problem in fact went back to the very foundation of the Dutch East India Company, which had become a self-perpetuating, self-justifying administrative system. The attempt to defend the idea of universal abstract law against local customary law was at the core of the legal controversy between the Utrecht School and the Leiden School. The doctrines of the Leiden scholars did not fit easily with the economic and administrative needs of empire or capitalist enterprise, and the romantic view of law was an implicit threat to Dutch authority in for example giving legitimacy to the indigenous process of adjustment. The Utrecht School claimed that customary adjustment as a restoration of communal harmony was clearly inferior to a rational legal system that demanded recognition of evil intention and balanced punishment with the scale of an offense. Any imperial power that recognized such irrational and ad hoc customary practices had simply forfeited its legitimate right to rule. As a result, too much scholarly attention was given to *adat* practices. In the ideological confrontation between these two positions, the technical debates about land rights, legal process, tort, and punishment were basically controversies over the issue of sovereignty. Whereas the function of the Leiden School had been to invent Indonesian nationhood, the Utrecht School sought to nurture the Dutch polity.

The same might be said of the functions of law in the Ottoman Empire, which also embraced many different traditions. The Ottoman system is of special interest to political sociologists because of the millet system in which different communities (essentially people of the book) enjoyed some degree of autonomy to practice their own religion and customs. It is often referred to as an early illustration, according to Will Kymlicka (1995), of the development of "group-differentiated rights" to cope with internal diversity and difference.[15] While the ulama attempted to impose the *Shari'a* on the state and society, they were often resisted by the ruling elite. The Ottoman legal system was "decentralized, diverse and dynamic to cope with the wide religious, ethnic and cultural diversity of the population."[16] It consisted of three components: *Shari'a*, *kanun* (including customary law), and the legal systems of minority communities in the millet system. Scholars have suggested that the separation between *Shari'a* and *kanun* laid the foundation for Turkish secularism. Turkey provides another historical example of legal pluralism in an imperial system but one very different obviously from either Britain or America.

In societies with many languages, cultures, and religions, it makes sociological sense to see them as federations of communities rather than as unified nation states. In empirical terms, not all states are as complex as Indonesia or as culturally diverse as the Ottoman Empire. Nation-states like France, England, and Germany are not postcolonial states like Indonesia. Federal states like the Commonwealth of Australia, the United States, and the United Kingdom are not like the Ottoman Empire. To misquote the famous phrase of Benedict Anderson (1983), some states are more "imagined" than others.[17] While the idea of state sovereignty and a unified legal code may be a political fiction, it seems to me that it is a necessary fiction or at least that any functional system of law would have to have some minimal agreement about a final umpire who could arbitrate between competing legal claims. The growth of legal pluralism becomes a problem in societies where a common citizenship is fragmenting under the impact of globalization and the decline of shared culture.

FOUR LEVELS OF *SHARI'A* ACTIVITY

In order to clarify this argument, we can usefully distinguish between four levels at which *Shari'a* might find a presence and function in a society whose constitutional arrangements are clearly secular. There could be firstly some formal institutional development of religious law in both civil and private matters; this development would involve some public recognition of religious courts, presumably under the final oversight of the state or some parliamentary institution. Secondly, there could be the development of religious arbitration, in which these "courts" are confined to private disputes (typically around marriage divorce, adoption, and so forth). If accepting religious law means in practice accepting third-party arbitration, then legal pluralism might not in itself be a direct or obvious threat to state sovereignty. However, for many critics, arbitration is merely the "thin end" of the legal wedge, raising the problem about whether an arbitration hearing is in fact a "court." Thirdly, there could be an informal and unregulated use of *Shari'a*, for example through the spread of "online fatwas" providing informal legal judgements and opinions about matters relating to how Muslims should live in a secular society, or offering to provide guidance in arbitration between conflicting parties. With the global spread of the Internet, some degree of informal but popular opinion-formation takes place between individuals in ways that may be compatible with *Shari'a* as a consensus-seeking legal tradition. This development involves not the formal institutionalization of religious law but an informal growth of religious codes into everyday life. The spread of veiling is one very obvious example of new forms of urban piety. Similarly, we can regard the demand for the implementation of the *Shari'a* as yet another aspect of new piety movements. The informal spread of *Shari'a* courts and appeals to *Shari'a* online judgements can be defined as the "*Shari'a*-ization of the everyday world." There are however, from the perspective of religious orthodoxy, some important questions surrounding such online legal opinions. The first is that Internet religious opinions can no longer be controlled by traditional religious authorities, and therefore there is an erosion of religious authority.[18] The second related problem is what we might call "fatwa shopping," namely the search for a particular religious opinion that will satisfy the specific requirements of an individual.

Finally, we can regard—as many Muslims do—the law in terms of a moral system and type of consciousness shaping everyday life, but not necessarily operating as a formal system of law. The idea of *Shari'a* as the basis of personal piety was defined by Marshall G. S. Hodgson in volume one of his *The Venture of Islam* as the piety of the learned (the ulama) that shaped the thought and practice of Muslim societies. Hodgson called this orientation "the Shariah-minded programme for private and public living centred on the Shariah law."[19] However, "it was probably only among the merchant classes that their ideals came close to overall fulfilment."[20] In volume two, Hodgson claimed that this "kergygmatic force of the Shariah-minded piety" had declined in favor of a more rigid and ritualistic approach to piety, namely what he called "paradigmatic-tracing piety."[21] In the long term it became the backbone of devotional life for the mass of Muslims. While modern reformers often want nostalgically to see the *Shari'a* law as the dominant and shared framework of public life, Hodgson offers us a more subtle way of thinking of *Shari'a* less as formal law and more as a framework for personal piety.

But why has this debate about the importance and role of the *Shari'a* emerged at this particular juncture? The obvious answer is that with globalization and mass migration of labor, more and more Muslims find themselves living in culturally alien environments where new questions constantly emerge about whether a particular practice, custom, or object is in fact compatible with being a good Muslim. The spread of urban piety in the Muslim heartland and beyond can be considered as a contemporary example of Hodgson's "Shariah-mindedness" or "*Shari'a*-consciousness," as I would describe this development not simply as a narrow manifestation of formal law but of a growing religious consciousness. The demand for *Shari'a* in the public domain has to be understood as an example of a deepening religious consciousness among urban, socially-mobile, and educated Muslims; it is not the consciousness of a traditional ulama but of new urban elites with Western degrees and a desire to reshape their lives by reference to such pious norms.

CULTURE AND EGALITARIANISM

These developments therefore raise a much deeper question about the centrality of *Shari'a* to orthodoxy or at least to traditional interpretations of orthodoxy. In addition, this issue brings us to the more important questions about what types of behaviors or beliefs can be accepted within a liberal, secular, and democratic society that allows for multiculturalism. Some of the most potent criticisms of multiculturalism were developed by Brian Barry (2001) in *Culture and Equality*.[22] As the subtitle of this work—*An Egalitarian Critique of Multiculturalism*—indicated, Barry was concerned that the modern enthusiasm for identity politics and cultural difference undermines the egalitarian principles that are essential to democracy and that the privileges ascribed to the special interests articulated by religious minorities could not be reconciled with considerations of justice. For example, in his critical commentary on the isolation of the Amish community and their immunities from state interference, Barry argued that any public acceptance of a religious practice of a minority could only be justified if it could be demonstrated that the practice was pivotal to the beliefs of that minority. He argues convincingly that many of the exemptions (from taxation, jury service, military service, and so forth) won by Amish communities are not essential to the practice of their faith and are inappropriately wrapped up in the language of freedom of religion and the Constitution. Furthermore, he questions whether societies like the Amish are in fact voluntary associations since the option of leaving the community is severely restricted. One might for example argue that in Christianity the Eucharist is pivotal to Christian belief and practice, whereas the rosary is not. Therefore any legal prohibition on the Eucharist might be unwarranted and a threat to the survival of the religion, but banning the use of the rosary in public would not be hugely damaging to Christian values. However, Barry's argument offers a much more stringent test for religious organizations because he argues that none of them really match up to the criteria established by liberal democracies—transparency, equality, voluntary membership, the rights of dissent, and legitimate opposition.

We could combine some aspects of Barry's criticism of multiculturalism with a position adopted by Jurgen Habermas following John Rawls' defense of liberal principles.[23] Habermas has proposed that in a postsecular society it behoves both secular and religious citizens to engage in a public defense of their beliefs.[24] It is not sufficient to say that humanism is self-evidently true or that religious revelation is beyond rational scrutiny and needs no justification. Communicative openness is a requirement of democratic norms in a public space and hence customs and beliefs have to be rationally justifiable. This rule applies to secular humanists and to fundamentalists alike.

This criterion of public rationality might provide us with a suitable approach to an analysis of *Shari'a* in public space. Satisfying this criterion is of course especially problematic in the case of religious beliefs and practices that may be justified by divine revelation rather than by secular reason. Nevertheless, the criterion prompts the following question: is the operation of *Shari'a* in the public domain a necessary and unquestionable basis for the religious life? This article broadly supports the arguments put forward by Ahmed An-Na'im that in fact secularization is paradoxically a necessary condition for the enjoyment of a religious life. An-Na'im shows that "[b]y its nature and purpose *Shari'a* can only be freely observed by believers; its principles lose their religious authority and value when enforced by the state. . . . the state has its proper functions, which may include adjudication among competing claims of religious and secular institutions, but it should be seen as a politically neutral institution performing necessarily secular functions, without claiming religious authority as such."[25] Similar arguments have been developed, for example, by the contemporary Iranian philosopher Abdulkarim Soroush (2000) who, embracing the ideals of secular liberalism, argues in favor of a conception of multiple democracies, including "religious democracy."[26]

From a sociological standpoint, secularization (by which I simply mean the neutrality of the state in its relationship with diverse religious traditions) is a necessary condition of civil harmony in culturally diverse societies. Secularization creates a public space in which *Shari'a* (along with other religious and legal traditions) can be accommodated by liberal democracies, provided there is ample opportunity for the exercise of public reasoning and provided that a number of conditions can be satisfied (such as gender equality, the sovereignty of a final arbiter, and so forth). An-Na'im supports this normative claim about secularization with a set of empirical examples from Turkey, India, and Indonesia, which underpin his historical argument that the restoration of the Caliphate and the universal imposition of *Shari'a* is not the sine qua non of Muslim piety. His position of course goes against the radical theology of political Islam that demands the restoration of the Caliphate and the universal imposition of the *Shari'a* in public life, requiring therefore the rejection of Western legal traditions.[27]

CITIZENSHIP AS THE FOUNDATION

I want to argue that the problem of legal pluralism lies elsewhere, namely that it contributes to the ongoing erosion of citizenship as a shared cultural, social, and political framework. Legal pluralism and multiculturalism require a lively and effective framework of active citizenship if they are to be successful. With the weakening of these common ties, separate religious schools, the growth of legal pluralism, the wearing of distinctive religious dress in public spaces, ethnic segregation, the development of symbolically segregated communities such as the proliferation of *eruv* in the Jewish world, and the consequent of unintended creation of parallel communities can only promote an acute differentiation of identity and have a divisive effect on society, leading to what I have elsewhere called "the enclave society." [28]

Within this a broader framework, one has to be sceptical about the survival of viable forms of citizenship, given the dominance of the market over both state and civil society. The decline in direct personal taxation, the disappearance of conscription, the general diminution of social capital, the decline of public institutions, and the weakness of the civil sphere have led to an erosion of a common experience of shared citizenship.[29] Religious differences and identities are often championed in the name of human rights, namely freedom of conscience. The paradox of these individual rights is that we need effective and viable states if rights are to be enforced and the enforcement of rights is a necessary condition of political life. Hence, despite much of the contemporary commentary about the decline of the state and the growth of porous political boundaries, we need to be concerned that any decline in the authority and coherence of the state—associated with neoliberal globalization and financial deregulation—will in fact undermine the political foundations that are necessary to sustain legal pluralism, multiculturalism, and participatory citizenship. The real political issue behind the possible growth of *Shari'a* arbitration is not (or not just) the conventional feminist anxiety about equal treatment of women, but a broader concern about the current state of citizenship in democracies. The notion that we have a right to choose the legal systems under which we are to be ruled in the name of cultural difference and multiculturalism makes little political sense and would destroy the very institutions that protect our cultural diversity.

Any discussion of citizenship will have to consider the relationships—and especially their changing relationships—between the state, the market, and civil society. At the outset, we should note that civil society is the site of active citizenship and the social foundation of any viable democracy. What we might call bottom-up or participatory citizenship emerges from the social movements and social struggles for rights in civil society rather than a form of top-down citizenship by the state. Durable and robust citizenship is also promoted by the presence of a cultural system that fosters public rather than private identities and upholds shared moral codes. In short, the idea of citizenship is central to any political discourse about rights, participation, and identity.

However, in modern social and political theory there is considerable criticism of the conventional assumptions of national citizenship because it thought to be too rigid and unable to embrace social diversity, especially the religious diversity emerging with global migration. Political critics have called for new categories such as flexible or semicitizenship.[30] For example, national citizenship is necessarily exclusive, and hence in modern societies there is an acute problem around both internal and external boundaries. By providing criteria of membership that determine access to shared resources, citizenship necessarily defines a boundary to society that excludes people who do not possess those criteria of full membership. This exclusionary aspect of citizenship has been criticized in the modern context because it cannot allegedly provide effective policies with respect to the complexities of migration. This contractual character of national citizenship has been questioned by critics who want to see a more open and flexible foundation for social rights emerging from the transformation of the territorial assumptions of national citizenship. For example, in *Genealogies of Citizenship*, Margaret Somers argues that "democratic citizenship regimes (including human rights) can thrive only to the extent that egalitarian and solidaristic principles, practices, and institutions of civil society and the public commons are able to act with equal force against the exclusionary threats of market-driven politics."[31] Given the connection between rights and territory, the ownership of a passport is therefore the critical issue in terms of mobility, employment, income level, and personal security. This issue of exclusion raises difficult problems, not only for stateless people, refugees and asylum seekers, but also for legal labor migrants who are denizens but without the full rights of citizens. It is suggested that traditional patterns of national citizenship need to be reformed around ideas of flexible citizenship to take account postnational sovereignty.[32]

While recognizing the difficulties associated with the legacy of T. H. Marshall (1950)[33] and the problems facing the global proletariat of migrants who possess no secure rights as mere denizens, I am not persuaded that we can so easily abandon the framework of national citizenship and national sovereignty. Despite the obvious globalization of the economy, the world is still composed primarily of nation-states with specific state interests. In order for individuals to enjoy effective participation in society, there has to be some mechanism for the distribution of resources and therefore the principal issue confronting citizenship is the general problem of scarcity. However, few contemporary discussions of either human rights or citizenship confront the problem of the scarcity of resources that are necessary to satisfy human needs. The whole literature on identity and cultural citizenship has remained oblivious to this fundamental economic problem. The wealth of societies necessary to support citizenship is often taken for granted, or scarcity is treated as an ideological construct invented by elites to discipline labor. In the current economic crisis, there are good reasons to believe that this generic problem is exacerbated by a variety of new conditions—economic slow down, outsourcing, aging populations, energy crises, rising food prices and energy prices, loss of biodiversity, civil instability, "new wars," and natural disasters such as the 2011 crises in Queensland (Australia), Brazil, Russia, and Sri Lanka. The contemporary task of national citizenship is to enhance the life chances of the majority of the population in a context of increasing global competition for scarce resources. The function of national citizenship has been to promote social equality through the (re)distribution of scarce resources. These functions of the state require an effective taxation system that is seen to be fair and impacts on all citizens. Taxation, rather like the rule of law, is essential to a modern democracy.[34] The taxation basis of the modern state has been eroded by the decline in personal taxation, the aging of the population, and the shrinkage of the working population. These taxation problems in part explain the contemporary erosion of state support for welfare benefits and state pensions, which have been traditional pillars of social citizenship.

ARGUMENTS FOR COMMON CITIZENSHIP

In the following discussion, I take a fairly pessimistic view that the preservation of cultural, religious, or legal differences can only be sustained if there is an overarching framework of citizenship that binds people together into a shared community. Without that commonality and a shared national project, there is a real danger that societies will break down into isolated enclaves or parallel societies in which communities with separate schools, with little spatial propinquity and retaining separate cultural traditions—and in this case their own legal traditions—will fragment. The wider society becomes simply a collection of gated communities and cultural enclaves. The problem of parallel communities is real, and it is not difficult to image the growth of modern societies dominated by global megacities in which there is relatively little shared civility. John Rawls in *The Law of Peoples* (1999) has spoken of the importance of an "overlapping consensus"[35] of fundamental doctrines if a liberal society is to survive, but such a liberal consensus cannot function without a system of overlapping social groups. Taking multiculturalism seriously may force us to take social solidarity seriously, namely to take a critical look at the celebration of difference at the cost of those things that hold us together. From a sociological point of view, multiculturalism without some powerful framework of shared interests and shared institutions cannot provide an adequate cultural framework for any complex society. More problematically there are powerful processes in modern societies that are undermining public life—neoliberal policies for the privatization of pensions, health care, and education, the powerful imprint of subjective individualism in consumer culture, the cultural dominance of private schools and universities, the loss of social capital with modern forms of communication, and the decline of social citizenship through the outsourcing of state functions.

Brian Barry argues that citizenship emerged out the long struggle to find a lasting settlement between Catholics and Protestants in Europe for people to live peacefully in society. While Kymlicka claims that the unitary republican model of citizenship can no longer respond effectively to the cultural and ethnic diversity of modern societies, Barry rejoins that "it is not at all apparent why it should not be up to the task of coping with religious and cultural differences now. . . . I maintain that the relatively peaceful incorporation of a wide range of religions and cultures in the past half century is a tribute to" the unitary model of secular citizenship.[36] The institutions of modern citizenship have been the principal mechanisms of social inclusion in contemporary society, and citizenship has played a major role in mitigating the negative consequences of the market. In particular, social citizenship is important in containing and reducing the negative consequences of social class differences in capitalism. Without these social rights, the history of Western capitalism in the twentieth century would have been a good deal more turbulent.

LAW AND LIBERALISM

The conflict in the West over the *Shari'a* is fast replacing the conflict over the veil as one of the most contested issues in Western liberal societies. From western Europe to Australia, various measures have been discussed in parliaments to ban the *burqa* from public spaces, and these proposals have received widespread public endorsement. A Pew Center Global Attitudes Project from May and June 2010 found that 82 percent of the French public were in favor of legislation to ban full veiling.[37] The debate about the veil can be regarded as an issue around cultural identity, but the question of the *Shari'a* is more controversial because it raises questions about national sovereignty, a unified legal system, and the framework of modern citizenship. In the United Kingdom, there has been considerable disquiet, expressed in the national press, that the government has adopted a pragmatic policy of de facto recognition of *Shari'a* courts and not just arbitration. For example, a *Sunday Times* report in September 2008 noted that "the government had quietly sanctioned the powers for sharia judges to rule on cases ranging from divorce and financial disputes to those involving domestic violence."[38] *Shari'a* court rulings can be enforced in terms of the Arbitration Act 1996 through the county courts or High Court. Under a system of "alternative dispute resolution," cases can be heard and judgements enforced where both parties have agreed to give the power of resolution to an arbitration tribunal.

In these cases, the *Shari'a* brings out an interesting contradiction in modern liberal democratic societies. Acceptance of the veil as a mode of religious dress and *Shari'a* as a legal framework for the conduct of both private and public matters exposes an important tension between individual human rights to freedom of religious belief and practice and the need to defend a common framework of citizenship against the divisive and fissiparous forces of societies that are subject to fragmentation through globalization and the dominance of the market over civil society.

From the perspective of the sociology of religion, *Shari'a* evolved as the legal framework of societies with a Muslim majority as the expression of a social consensus within the community. The problem for modern Muslims living as diasporic communities (and typically therefore as minority communities) as a result of worldwide migration is that achieving a consensus about how to live as a good Muslim in modern societies has become problematic. It is problematical for at least two reasons. Firstly, new situations emerge. Can a female Muslim living in Germany join a secular football team, and if so what should she wear? Secondly, much of this debate occurs online with new sources of authority and therefore outside the traditional framework of communal consensus. Hence it is unclear who has authority to speak on such matters. From the perspective of the sociology of law, I want to propose that the total collection of Internet activity (blogs, Facebook, YouTube, Twitter, and so forth) within the diaspora constitutes a new type of Muslim consensus, but it is an emergent consensus outside the normal or traditional framework. In one sense, because Islam lacks a centralized authority system, the global Internet is the Muslim community or *ummah*.

An informal or populist version of Islamic law may in fact challenge the authority of traditional forms of religious authority. In attempting to understand the current situation of Muslim minorities, it is important to focus on actual practice rather than on formal systems of belief. What constitutes Muslim belief cannot be found in sociological terms by reading the official texts; it can only be found by observing everyday Muslim practice. For example, what constitutes piety for contemporary Muslims cannot be grasped simply through a study of the Qur'an. We might take as an example the question as to whether a good Muslim could have a tattoo or some other body modification. Qur'anic sources and *hadith* tell us little about piercing, tattooing, and other aspects of popular youth culture. According to the *hadith* (customary teaching), God has made human beings perfect, and therefore it is a blasphemy to change the human form. If one examines online discussions about tattoos among young Muslims, there are interesting problems thrown up about the issue. For example, is the use of henna also prohibited? If one already has tattoos before conversion to Islam, is it important to undergo surgery to have them removed? It appears that some young Muslims are already experimenting with tattoos and jewelry that have what one might call Islamic themes. There is an equally lively and dense debate about appropriate sexual behavior—homosexuality, polygamy, and gender roles—among young Muslims online. In diasporic communities, this question is typically resolved through online discussion. Where there is an emerging modern consensus in popular discourse about body modifications, then the online discussion functions as an emerging communal consensus about good practice. These discussions can begin to assume the same role or function as a fatwa but not of a traditional or customary judgement. There is already therefore an informal and local set of online norms on guiding Muslims toward pious behaviors that have a quasi-legal status. We might invent a concept to describe this evolutionary development of custom through localized, communal judgements as a process of de facto "*Shari'a*-ization."

RELIGIOUS COURTS: THE PROBLEM OF ARBITRATION

This growth of an informal set of customary norms is of course very different from the creation of formal arbitration courts. In this respect, the objections to accepting *Shari'a* have already emerged, for example, in legal debate in Ontario, Canada where from 1991 onward the secular courts authorized the use of *Shari'a* in civil arbitrations over divorce, child custody, and inheritance cases. The Arbitration Act allowed individuals to access religiously based tribunals within the province. The Act was in part a response to an over-burdened legal system for which the creation of these arrangements would address these administrative problems. These provisions included not only recognition of Islamic legal traditions but also the legal legacy of rabbinical, Catholic, and aboriginal faiths. These legal developments gave rise to concern not only among secular Canadians but among Muslim migrants to Canada.

The arguments against such arbitration arrangements that were reported in the *Globe and Mail* included the fact that many Muslim women are poorly educated and consequently do not easily understand their rights under Canadian law. The imams can make judgments where there is no oversight, and as a result how would one know whether they contravened the secular law? Because the women are often living in social enclaves where there is little understanding of women's rights and gender equality, they are vulnerable and may not be able to access third-party oversight. These debates were aggravated by sensational reporting of a murder case in which a young girl aged 16 years from a Toronto suburb was strangled to death by her father following her refusal to wear a head scarf. These arbitration arrangements were criticized not only by secular groups but also by the Canadian Council of Muslim Women.

In response to the debate and the problems it threw up, Premier Dalton McGuinty determined to repeal the Act without prior discussion with his Cabinet. The issue has been explosive within the public domain. In August 2005 Ayaan Hirsi Ali attended a conference in Toronto in support of Homa Arjomand, the coordinator of the International Campaign Against *Shari'a* Courts in Canada. On September 2005 McGuinty announced that "sharia arbitration in family law matters" would be banned from the province. Those groups that supported the arbitration arrangements argued that the ban prevented religious women from living "a faith-based life."[39] However, in my view this defense of arbitration courts confuses the conditions that make possible *Shari'a*-mindedness and the presence or availability of arbitration in religious courts.

CONCLUSION: PUBLIC REASON, FORMAL LAW, AND *SHARI'A*-CONSCIOUSNESS

In a functioning secular democracy, any system of religious laws would have to satisfy the tests of liberalism and egalitarianism that were developed by Barry in *Culture & Equality*. These criteria include the notion that if religious organizations are genuinely *voluntary associations*, then individuals must have the right to opt out. This norm would apply equally across the board from Amish to Muslim and to Jewish associations. Regrettably the public debate around the notion of apostasy in Islam has often been inflamed by anger around such publications as Ayaan Hirsi Ali's *Infidel* (2007).[40] The principle that individuals can opt out of their own communities is perhaps the most problematic from the perspective of an ethnic minority that believes it is besieged by the culture of the dominant group. In the case of ethnic minorities, the survival of their cultures and traditions requires some degree of continuity of socialization and cultural transmission. Since we get our culture along with our mother's milk, the coherence of social groups rests heavily on a process that has historically depended on women. Hence, women are typically subject to excessive and often brutal subordination to group norms. But this sociological fact of course offers no normative reason for supporting gender inequalities, let alone domestic violence.

The further technical problem with any discussion of *Shari'a* in modern societies is the unresolved legal dispute about whether *Shari'a* arbitration courts are in fact courts of law. It is clear that Muslim arbitration is fairly widespread in secular societies—alongside similar Jewish arbitration courts and Catholic cannon courts. In England, the *Telegraph* newspaper reported on September 14, 2008 that *Shari'a* courts had been operating since August 2007 under the Arbitration Act in many English cities where there are substantial Muslim communities.[41] In Britain, arbitration can be carried out by any two adult persons if they have volunteered to have their case heard by a tribunal. The statute simply requires them to sign an arbitration agreement before the proceedings take place. The arbitration can be conducted in accordance with any rules or legal system that is specified in the arbitration agreement, including *Shari'a*. The final judgement or decision is registered with a civil court and enforced by such a court as if the "trial" had taken place in a civil court. The system of Muslim tribunals in Britain is in line with separate mediation for Anglican and Jewish communities.

With respect to the operation of *Shari'a* courts under the Arbitration Act, there can be little to criticize in the development of arbitration tribunals provided they function within the provisions of the Act, and they have given rise to significant public dispute in Britain and more generally in Europe. The right-wing Dutch politician Geert Wilders has attempted to spread an anti-Muslim movement in Britain and America to prevent such developments. In the United States, similar arbitration arrangements are also available through the US Federal Arbitration Act (FAA) of 1925, which provides for the resolution of disputes arising out of private contractual relationships by an arbitration panel. As in Britain, where there is a substantive difference between *Shari'a* and state or federal law, then clearly the judgement of an arbitrator could not be legally enforced.

However, what is at issue here is not just a technical debate about the notion of arbitration. What is at stake is the issue of sovereignty and citizenship. In this respect Stanley Diamond's distinction between "order of custom" and "order of law" is useful in clarifying our discussion.[42] While ordinary citizens may not be able to define sovereignty or state, they have to respect the function of the law to (1) exercise superior authority within its compass to all other parties that are brought before it; (2) to operate with neutrality and disinterest; and (3) to deliver regular, stable, and predictable decisions. Provided these conditions are fulfilled, ordinary citizens know where to find the law, and they can respect its authority.

It is for these reasons that I have argued that the problems associated with *Shari'a* in fact lie elsewhere, namely with the changing nature of citizenship in modern societies. There is a danger that the formal recognition of religious laws in general and *Shari'a* in particular would contribute to a further fragmentation of modern societies—which are already deeply divided and low on trust. Multiculturalism, open borders, and positive attitudes toward migration have all been questioned and shaken in liberal societies by a lethal combination of terrorism, financial crisis, and economic downturn. If we were to extend multiculturalism to recognize *Shari'a* courts (or any other religious courts), then we would need to invest in many more processes to sustain some form of common citizenship. Acceptance of a public role for the *Shari'a* provides an acid test for the criteria of postsecularism that have been outlined in Habermas's recent work. In a democratic society, secular citizens have to offer public reasons for their political statements and attitudes, because "only in this way can political power shed its repressive character."[43] At the same time, religious citizens must be able to reflect objectively on their religious convictions and connect them with life in a secular society. In this discussion of "pubic reason," Habermas has developed John Rawls's *Political Liberalism* (1993)[44] by introducing his own version of deliberation as the cornerstone of democracy. A similar view is embraced by Amartya Sen in *The Idea of Justice* (2009)[45] in which he considers the empirical limitations on deliberative democracy such as the failures of the media and the press to provide critical views and objective knowledge about modern conditions.

Although Rawls, Habermas, and Sen have made major contributions to the theory of democracy, their understanding of the *sociological* conditions of critical debate is often underdeveloped. The key problem is how, in Rawls's terms, we can achieve a consensus in modern political systems. The assumption running through this article is that divisions between religions in a globalizing context have increased rather than diminished, and there is a danger that multicultural societies will become enclave societies. A philosophical consensus about constitutional principles or postsecular values is very different from a general social consensus. An overlapping consensus requires overlapping social groups—the product of high levels of intermarriage, common experiences, a shared welfare system, and a common school system. The growth of parallel communities undermines the prospect of overlapping social groups.

Without social solidarity an overlapping consensus is unlikely, and there is a danger of increasing social fragmentation and division.

In the meantime, the sociological fact is that *Shari'a* is already operating in modern secular societies wherever third-party adjudication of disputes takes place according to religious norms. In addition, there are major changes taking place within Muslim communities about the norms that are appropriate to living in a secular society. These Internet debates already transcend local or national jurisdictions, but they also transcend all forms of traditional debate. These small changes may be an indication of an emerging vernacular cosmopolitanism that may be, in the long run, a basis for engaging in debates, namely participating in public reasoning. These developments open up the possibility that what Marshall Hodgson called "Shari'ah-mindedness"[46] might be a source of religious understanding outside the formal legal framework as a site of cultural engagement.

NOTES

1. Rowan Williams, *Civil and Religious Law in England: A Religious Perspective. Foundation Lecture at the Royal Courts of Justice, Archbishop of Canterbury*, 2008, http://www.archbishopofcanterbury.org

2. Joseph Schacht Schacht, *Introduction to Islamic Law* (London: Routledge and Kegan Paul, 1964).

3. Michael Peletz, *Islamic Modern: Religious Courts and Cultural Politics in Malaysia* (Princeton: Princeton University Press, 2002).

4. Max Weber, *Economy and Society*, 2 vols. (Berkeley: University of California Press, 1978).

5. Abdullahi Ahmed An-Na'im, *Islam and the Secular State: Negotiating the Future of Shari'a* (Cambridge, MA: Harvard University Press, 2008).

6. Peter Burns, *The Leiden Legacy: Concepts of Law in Indonesia* (Leiden: KITLV Press, 2004), 255.

7. Brian Z. Tamanaha, "Understanding Legal Pluralism: Past to Present, Local to Global," *Sydney Law Review* 30 (2008): 375.

8. Brian Z. Tamanaha, *Realistic Socio-Legal Theory. Pragmatism and a Social Theory of Law* (Oxford: Clarendon Press, 1997), 9.

9. Michael Kemper and Maurus Reinkowski, eds., *Rechtspluralismus in der Islamischen Welt* (Berlin: Peter de Gruyter, 2005).

10. Burns, *The Leiden Legacy*.

11. Rachel Sieder, "Introduction," *Multiculturalism in Latin America: Indigenous Rights, Diversity and Democracy*, ed. Rachel Sieder (Houndmills, Basingstoke: Palgrave/Macmillan, 2002), 1–23.

12. Maryam Namazie, Yassi Atasheen, and Ann Waters, *Sharis Law in Britain. A Threat to One Law for All and Equal Rights* (London: One Law for All, 2010).

13. Keebet von Benda-Beckman, *Broken Stairways to Consensus: Village Justice and State Courts in Minangkabau* (Dordrecht: Foris, 1984).

14. Cornelis van Vollenhoven, Miskenningen van het adatrecht. Vier voordrachten aan de Nederlandsch-Indische Bestuuracademie (Leiden: Brill, 1909).

15. Will Kymlicka, *Multicultural Citizenship. A Liberal Theory of Minority Rights* (Oxford: Clarendon Press, 1995).

16. An-Na'im, *Islam and the Secular State*, 188.

17. Benedict Anderson, *Imagined Communities: Reflections on the Origins and Spread of Nationalism* (London and New York: Verso, 1983).

18. Bryan S. Turner, "Religious Authority and the New Media," *Theory Culture & Society* 24, no. 2 (2007): 117–34; Bryan S. Turner (with F. Vopli), "Introduction: Making Islamic Authority Matter," *Theory Culture & Society* 24, no. 2 (2007): 1–19.

19. Marshall G. S. Hodgson, *The Venture of Islam: Conscience and History in a World Civilization*, 3 vols. (Chicago: University of Chicago Press, 1974), 1:238.

20. Ibid.

21. Hodgson, *The Venture of Islam*, 2:179.

22. Brian Barry, *Culture and Equality: An Egalitarian Critique of Multiculturalism* (Cambridge, MA: Harvard University Press, 2001).

23. John Rawls, *Political Liberalism* (New York: Columbia University Press, 2003).

24. Jurgen Habermas and Eduardo Mendieta, *Religion and Rationality: Essays on Reason, God, and Modernity* (Cambridge, MA: MIT Press, 2002).

25. An-Na'im, *Islam and the Secular State*, 4.

26. Abdulkarim Soroush, *Reason, Freedom and Democracy in Islam* (Oxford: Oxford University Press, 2000).

27. Gilles Kepel, *The War for Muslim Minds: Islam and the West* (Cambridge, MA: The Belknap Press of Harvard University Press, 2004).

28. Bryan S. Turner, "The Enclave Society: Towards a Sociology of Immobility," *European Journal of Social Theory* 10, no. 2 (2007): 287–303.

29. Bryan S. Turner, "The Erosion of Citizenship," *British Journal of Sociology* 52, no. 2 (2001): 189–209.

30. Elizabeth Cohen, *Semi-Citizenship in Democratic Politics* (Cambridge: Cambridge University Press, 2009).

31. Margaret R. Somers, *Genealogies of Citizenship: Markets, Statelessness and the Right to Have Rights* (Cambridge: Cambridge University Press, 2008), 8.

32. Aihwa Ong, "Please Stay: Pied-a-Terre Subjects in the Megacity," in *Citizenship Between Past and Future*, ed. Engin F. Isin, Peter Nyers, and Bryan S. Turner (London: Routledge, 2008), 81–91.

33. T. H. Marshall, *Citizenship and Social Class and Other Essays* (Cambridge: Cambridge University Press, 1950).

34. Sven Steinmo, *Taxation and Democracy: Swedish, British and American Approaches to Financing the Modern State* (New Haven: Yale University Press, 1993).

35. John Rawls, *The Law of Peoples* (Cambridge, MA: Harvard University Press, 1999).

36. Barry, *Culture and Equality*, 21.

37. Pew Global Attitudes Project, *Widespread Support for Banning Full Islamic Veil in Western Europe*, July 8, 2010, http://www.pewresearch.org/pubs/1658/widespread-support-for-banning-full-islamic-veil-western-europe-not-in-america (accessed July 8, 2010).

38. Abul Taher, "Revealed: UK's First Official Sharia Courts," *The Sunday Times*, September 14, 2008.

39. Natasha Bakht, "Were Muslim Barbarians Really Knocking on the Gates of Ontario? The Religious Arbitration Controversy—Another Perspective," *Ottawa Law Review* 40 (2006): 71.

40. Ayaan Hirsi Ali, *Infidel* (New York: Free Press, 2007).

41. Richard Edwards, "Shari'a Courts Operating in Britain," *Telegraph*, September 14, 2008.

42. Stanley Diamond, "The Rule of Law Versus the Order of Custom," *Social Research* 38 (1971): 42–72.

43. Jurgen Habermas, *Between Naturalism and Religion* (Cambridge, UK: Polity), 122.

44. Rawls, *Political Liberalism*.

45. Amartya Sen, *The Idea of Justice* (Cambridge, MA: Belknap Press/Harvard University Press, 2009).

46. Hodgson, *The Venture of Islam*.

Legal Pluralism, Family Personal Laws, and the Rejection of *Shari'a* in Australia: A Case of Multiple or "Clashing" Modernities?

Malcolm Voyce[1] and Adam Possamai[2]

[1]Law School, Macquarie University, Australia
[2]Law School, University of Western Sydney, Australia

In some Western countries with Muslim minorities, there has been debate in the last few years about the role of *Shari'a* in the context of domestic family law. In Australia there has been a negative response to the adoption of *Shari'a*, as this form of law has been seen as divisive, patriarchal, and inconsistent with the notion of the rule of law. Underlying these responses to *Shari'a* has been the implication that Islamic law was/is backward and patriarchal whereas Western law was/is both secular and egalitarian. The aim of this article is to do three things: first, to show the extent to which matrimonial settlements by Muslims in divorce cases reflect a variety of personal practices and strategies toward *Shari'a* and Australian family law; second, to examine the values of Australian law and how law as a "form of practice" excludes Muslim values; and third, to situate this debate within the multiple modernity thesis and argue that, to move the matter further, we should look into working toward a new multifaith pragmatic modern project.

INTRODUCTION

In some Western countries with Muslim minorities, there has been debate in the last few years about the role of *Shari'a* in the context of domestic family law.[1] Specifically in Australia, there has been a negative response to the adoption of *Shari'a*, as this form of law has been seen as divisive, patriarchal, and inconsistent with the notion of the rule of law.[2] Underlying these reservations about *Shari'a* is the implication that Islamic law was/is backward and patriarchal, whereas Western law was/is secular and egalitarian. Some of the concerns of social commentators have been about the position of women in Islam; women are seen to be subject to oppressive practices and to general discrimination.[3]

The aim of this article is tripartite. First, it aims to show the extent to which matrimonial settlements by Muslims in divorce cases reflect a variety of personal practices and strategies toward both *Shari'a* and Australian family law. Second, it aims to briefly examine the values of Australian law and how law as a "form of practice" excludes Muslim values. Third, because of this practice of exclusion, and following the multiple modernity thesis (see below), the article wonders whether Australia is experiencing a "clash" of modernities, or rather a diversity of modernities.

Two premises underpin our research. First, the project aims to deconstruct the idea of a single interpretation of *Shari'a* in the Muslim communities of Australia. Rather than seeing *Shari'a* as being a monolithic system of detailed enactments that are immutable and invariable, we follow the approach that sees *Shari'a* as consisting of universal principles within a specialized framework for their actualization in human history.[4] Though *Shari'a* is often referred to in popular discourse as a universal code, it is often not applied as such, but rather implemented or concretized in the hands of traditional jurists.[5] This approach reflects the view that "there are as many Islams as there are situations to sustain it."[6] Second, we seek to locate the actual workings of the Australian Family Law Act 1975 (Cth) within Muslim communities and how the norms of this legislation shape family arrangements in the sense that parties might formulate their agreements in the shadow of the law.

This article is part of two larger projects that seek (1) to build a nuanced analysis of state family law as a site of negotiations around community values, and (2) to understand the processes of desecularization (or resecularization) in Australia following the recent theories of multiple modernities. The project will thus describe how the contemporary state family law of Australia accommodates diversity and plurality of family arrangements in the broader context of postsecularism in Australia. By postsecularism, we refer to the process of the deprivatization of religion and to the current dialogue about the management of the presence of religious groups within secular frameworks in the public sphere. As Habermas has underlined, the challenge today is to draw the "delimitations between a positive liberty to practise a religion of one's own and the negative liberty to remain spared from the religious practice of the others."[7] In other words, how do we work with postsecular societies' religious toleration in ways that celebrate religious diversity but that do not foreclose upon the freedom to be atheist? And, more specifically to this article, how far should our own and others' religious practices be implicated within the legal system?

THE BACKGROUND

Australia's Muslim community is small and consists of 340,392 people, which is 1.7 percent of the total population.[8] Australia has received immigrants at different time periods from countries experiencing a variety of reactions to Islamic resurgence. Substantial migration of Muslims to Australia began in the early 1970s, hence the majority of migrants are recent. While the Muslim population in Sydney comes from more than 60 different countries, there are large groups of people from Turkey and Lebanon.

Since 9/11 and the Bali bombings the role of Islam in Australian society has been the subject of much debate. Central to the debate about Muslim identity has been the issue of women's rights under Islam and the role of *Shari'a*. The debate has also concentrated on issues such as planning permissions for Muslim schools, controversy about "gang" rapes, and *Shari'a* as regards family law matters. There have been controversial comments by Muslim clerics, often involving disparaging comments about women. All these factors have resulted in Muslims becoming victims of discrimination, harassment, and racial profiling.[9] Debates over national security have brought into focus the issue of community acceptance of Muslims.[10]

While the Archbishop's speech in the United Kingdom[11] was widely reported in Australia, a full national debate about *Shari'a* never really developed. The notion of adoption or assimilation of *Shari'a* was rejected outright with no explanation or discussion as to its particular attributes or how it actually operated in practice. While the Coalition Government (comprising the Liberal and National parties) were in office, Prime Minister John Howard (1996–2007) attempted to gain political support by condemning *Shari'a*.[12] In a post-9/11 atmosphere Howard seemed to consider it unwise to be associated with Islamic values and that, in any event, it would go against his strong political lines on "law and order" and Islamic threat to say anything positive about *Shari'a*. On assuming office in 2007, the new Labour Party leader Kevin Rudd also made comments about not being prepared to recognize *Shari'a*.[13]

THE FAMILY LAW ACT 1975 (CTH) AND LEGAL PLURALISM

Some countries have adopted a system of legal pluralism. Legal pluralism is the system of law that allows for more than one legal system to operate within one jurisdiction at the same time.[14] One expression of legal pluralism conceives that separate personal laws may operate in the areas of family law. A personal law system may be defined as a system in which each individual is subject to the jurisdiction of his/her own religio-legal norms and institutions with regard to matters of marriage, maintenance, custody of children, and inheritance. In such a system a Muslim may be subject to *Shari'a*, or a Jew subject to Halakhah.

In Australia there is one nationwide system of law and no form of legal pluralism in the area of personal law. The Australian Law Reform Commission issued a report that recommended that indigenous laws be recognized in the family law area, but stopped short of recommending separate indigenous legal mechanisms for indigenous communities.[15] However, this report has been ignored, and its recommendations have not been implemented. A later report from Western Australia on the recognition of customary law warned against the recognition, concluding that the operation of two separate systems of law would have a divisive outcome.[16]

Another report by the Australian Law Reform Commission advocated a path toward recognition of multiculturalism through the removal of procedural barriers and enhancement of cross-cultural awareness. It did not support the idea that there should be special laws constructed around ethnic identities; this idea detracted from what it saw as the necessity that laws express "equality and universality."[17] However, research such as that by Humphrey[18] discovered that, for example, some Lebanese groups did not see Australian law as expressing "equality and universality," but as another political arena that was partisan and manipulable. In this sense, legal decisions were seen by some at that time to be lacking in legitimacy.

In general Australian governments have rejected the adoption of personal laws for religious or aboriginal groups. The Family Law Act 1975 (Cth) in Australia is commonly regarded as a progressive law guaranteeing gender justice. The principles of no-fault divorce under this law, for example, usually allow for equal sharing of property. This sharing of the resources of a marriage signifies the recognition of the homemaking contribution of both parties.

The notion of legal pluralism in another sense allows us to envisage how nonformal dispute mechanisms may operate beyond the formal scope of legal codes. In some cases customary or personal religious "laws" or ways of proceeding may not have formal recognition by the state. Under a wider view of law and legal pluralism we may see these (customary) practices as legal under such a view of law; law may be seen as a body of regularized procedures and normative standards, considered justiciable in any group, which contributes to the creation and prevention of disputes and their settlement through argumentative discourse coupled with the threat of force. This approach allows us to consider the decisions of *Shari'a* councils as "legal" arrangements.

SHARI'A IN AUSTRALIA

While Islamic law is not official in Australia, it nevertheless informs the ideas and conduct of Muslim communities. It is beyond the scope of this article to give an exposition of Islamic family law.[19] Such an exposition would involve treatment of this topic in a variety of angles that recognize *Shari'a* or incorporate some of its values. A general coverage of Islamic law as regards marriage would mention the legal effects that arise from the solemnization of a valid Muslim marriage, the grounds for divorce, the extent of a husband's control over his wife, the elements of a marriage contract, the entitlement to maintenance, the ownership of property, and inheritance rights.

Furthermore, it is beyond the scope of this article to describe migrants' ideas of *Shari'a* derived from their various countries of departure. These expectations are important as they influence family settlements. They invoke the concept of the operation of "transborder citizenship," whereby immigrants choose to live their lives across borders while maintaining social relationships and ideas of law from other nation states.[20] As we have indicated, Australian Islamic law, as a unified law across ethnic divisions, does not exist, but in the minds of some Muslims it has a living reality. In addition, many Muslims have problems with their lack of familiarity with the existing Australian legal system, the adversarial nature of the court system, the unsympathetic nature of many judicial officials, and the areas of law relating to property, domestic violence, and custody.[21]

One of the features of Islamic family law that we wish to note here is that Islam allows no separation of the social spheres (in the Luhmannien sense) and therefore applies no differentiation of political and religious authority. Islam is a complete system of living that perceives life as an integrated whole. Family law is central and of eternal value to the *Shari'a*. Its rules are seen as comprehensive in the sense that, contrary to divine intervention, human intervention is seen as limited in application.[22]

Modern criticism of *Shari'a* has revolved around the practice of polygamy, the power of the husband to terminate the marriage contract (and the lack of the wife's similar right), and the husband's rights over his wife and children. In this context, a traditional Islamic position on women's rights during and after marriage gives women lesser rights than men.[23] A persistent idea among Muslim men *and* women seems to be that according to Islamic rules in divorce settlements, matrimonial fault should be taken into account and that the men should receive the larger share of the property.[24]

Reforms in some countries (e.g. Turkey) have been subject to the criticism that changes in the law based on Western ideals have gone too far and have ignored the aspirations of Muslim communities. The question then arises: how should Western states respond to a reassertion of Islam? Rather than seeing Islam as a monolith notion, as a product of European bias,[25] or as a form of essentialism, the authors of this article see Islam as containing a number of cluster attributes that may be reworked and articulated within any community. Perhaps "resurgence" may be seen, not as a retreat into a traditional and conservative interpretation of Islam, but rather as an innovative reworking of texts.[26] While it is unlikely that reforms in Western states would allow child marriages, polygamy, and the undermining of the equalization of entitlements between husband and wife upon divorce, some states in Canada and the UK[27] have begun to debate the notion of law reform as regards recognition of *Shari'a* in the areas of divorce and maintenance.

In Australia some Islamic groups have set up a Board of Imams to deal with various family matters such as divorce, property, and children. These bodies follow *Shari'a* principles together with a selective use of Australian law.

What is the nature of these bodies? Do they construct a "parallel system of law,"[28] are such imams providing counseling/advice, and/or are they carrying out mediations within families in dispute? In exploring this alternative system we here recognize that the mediation process might be fraught with power inequalities and, in reality, the process may be one of arbitration in which a decision is imposed.

Rather than talk of a parallel court structure, it is more appropriate to speak of the operation of the Board of Imams as a hybridist system. We see this hybridist system as consisting of the mediation and arbitration processes and in some cases the handing down of judgments, all these processes taking place in the shadow of the law. The parties involved negotiate their problems around their various understandings of *Shari'a* and their respective understandings of what Australian family law may be on any given issue. Krayem[29] reports that, in Sydney, most imams grant religious divorces in circumstances where the husband is absent or will not cooperate. She reports that imams are conscious that they are operating in the context of Australian family law and that what they recommend might only be a first step in a longer legal process.

Why do Muslims consult imams as regards divorce? The answer is that many Muslims feel that an appropriate way must be found to end a marriage that is culturally meaningful and fits with the Islamic faith and cultural values.[30] Some Muslims report that they would not feel really divorced unless they were divorced religiously.[31] At the same time, many Muslims wish their divorce to be resolved by Australian law.

In Australia and overseas, several criticisms have been made of *Shari'a* councils. One is that *Shari'a* procedures disadvantage women, who may suffer intimidation or be unable to give full consent to processes applied. The criticism is that women may suffer rejection or lower esteem from their community should they not adhere to *Shari'a* findings.[32] A second criticism of such informal justice systems is that they may result in "imam shopping," or indeed that consulting an imam is the first step in "forum shopping."[33] (While the seeking of alternative venues has been seen as a negative, we do not see it as such, as most litigants in any dispute look for appropriate venues either inside or outside the system.) A third criticism of *Shari'a* councils is that their decisions create a form of personal law that contradicts the idea that all subjects in a state should adhere to one law—the claim that law should be universal, that the central state should provide complete and comprehensive dispute procedures for all citizens, and that hybrid rules and practices will dilute the value of an universal law.[34] However, the Australian Family Law Act allows a considerable amount of plurality in practice, and it has been argued that group differentiated rights do assist individual well-being and that such rights are not antithetical to liberal democracy.[35] Unequal treatment does not automatically make a set of unjust laws.[36]

Further, discussion of authority in Islam should be underpinned by the realization that the debate over the opening of the gate of interpretation (*ijtihad*) in modern Islam has produced not a restoration of tradition, but a modernization of Islamic legal thinking and practice. In short, attempts to impose or implement *Shari'a* in postcolonial and multicultural contexts have brought out a more general debate within the Muslim community over the relevance and nature of Islamic legal custom. Because of the weak institutionalization of religious hierarchies in most Islamic settings, the legal debate over authority becomes localized, devolved, and fissiparous. Modern communications technologies have greatly facilitated this global legal discussion, but it is difficult to impose any transnational authority over situations where local mullahs pass legal judgments on Web sites for an audience that has no clear cultural or spatial boundary. The fundamentalist or maximal view that *Shari'a* should have some sort of monopoly or definite authority becomes very problematic in a context of legal pluralism, especially in diasporic communities where innovation is an inevitable outcome of migration and cultural adaptation.[37]

A "CLASH" OR A DIVERSITY OF MODERNITIES IN AUSTRALIA?

Recent sociological theories of religion[38] have adapted Eisenstadt's (2000) multiple modernities paradigm to the postsecularization thesis. Eisenstadt described this paradigm in cultural terms:

> The idea of multiple modernities presumes that the best way to understand the contemporary world—indeed to explain the history of modernity—is to see it as a story of continual constitution and reconstitution of a multiplicity of cultural programs. These ongoing reconstructions of multiple institutional and ideological patterns are carried forward by specific social actors in close connection with social, political, and intellectual activists, and also by social movements pursuing different programs of modernity, holding very different views of what makes societies modern.[39]

Eisenstadt's notion of multiple modernities is conceptually useful because it underlines the possibility that postsecularism can assume different forms cross-culturally. For example, Casanova[40] and Davie[41] differentiate the European case from that of the United States. This contrast between the European and US cases is instructive; both Europe and the US have gone through modernization processes that have differently affected their post-secularisms. Earlier, Davie[42] put Europe and the US at the extremes of a continuum. She described the European case in terms of state or elite control of religion (in which there is a culture of obligation, e.g., going to Church because one must), and the US case as that of religious voluntarism (in which there is a culture of consumption or choice). Davie[43] observed that, on this continuum between religious obligation and religious voluntarism, Europe is slowly shifting toward voluntarism. Along this continuum, Australia is a hybrid case.[44] These observations are notable for the attention they draw to the different cultures of these countries and the effects of culture upon belief and nonbelief. Specifically, Davie draws attention to varied cultures of individualism, which are palpable in an age of neoliberalism, and how individualisms generate different national patterns of belief, adherence, and commitment.

Given the temporal and spatial international variations in belief and nonbelief, we might expect Australia and its modern project to be undergoing a process of postsecularism.[45] There is in fact increased decentralization, pluralism, and voluntarism of religious life within Australia, but these are not necessarily signs of religion's demise; rather, they may be processes of social dynamism and vitality.

Bouma[46] has recently claimed that, for Australians, religion must be a "low-temperature" phenomenon. By this he means that religion is not something Australians get overtly enthusiastic about and that Australian culture will prevent Australia from moving towards the US model. Bouma states, "it is not characteristically Australian to trumpet encounters with the spiritual like some American televangelists."[47] Bouma aptly describes the Australian soul in terms of religion and spirituality as "a shy hope in the heart." In coining this phrase, he was influenced by Manning Clarke's description of the ANZAC spirit as "a whisper in the mind and a shy hope in the heart."

> A shy hope in the heart aptly expresses the nature of Australian religion and spirituality. There is a profound shyness—yet a deeply grounded hope—held tenderly in the heart, in the heart of Australia. . . . Australians hold the spiritual gently in their hearts, speaking tentatively about it. The spiritual is treated as sacred. What is held protectively in the heart is sacred; the sacred is handled with great care. Not all things that evoke awe and wonder are loud and noisy, brassy and for sale.[48]

The development of secularization and its possible retreat have been characterized as temporally variable, with ebbs and flows. This "fussiness" of trends in religious belief and nonbelief constitutes what we mean by "postsecularism" in this research. Even global influences, such as neoliberalism and modernist enlightenment philosophy, are "worked out" differently in each society. Australia's postsecularism is complicated and involves unique contradictions and subtleties. It is a consequence of local cultures of individualism and indifference, the histories of religious establishment and the constitutional settings on faith, as well as contemporary open immigration (where there are no proscriptions or prescriptions regarding the faiths of applicants).

Taking into account the multiple modernities thesis we could argue that, with regard to *Shari'a*, there is a tension between the established secular and post-Christian modernity of Australia and currently growing Australian Muslim modernity. Many commentators might argue that *Shari'a* in Australia might be seen as premodern in the sense that it is not codified in a universal (or Western) way, or subject to the same process that legal systems have undergone in the Western world. *Shari'a*, it could be argued, has not gone through the same (so-called) full process of modernity, which is a process of differentiation between law and religion characteristic of post-Westphalian societies. According to Luhmann,[49] what characterizes the core of the modernization process is the differentiation between various social and cultural spheres of which religion is no longer the overarching, all-encompassing sphere (e.g., religion influencing law), but one among many (religion and law being different, relatively self-regulating spheres). How can such a process be said to be applied to *Shari'a*—as in *Shari'a*'s context, religion is the all-embracing sphere that includes the law? Could a different type of modernity be constructed without a differentiation between spheres, or do we have to expect that such differentiation is mandatory even in Islamic modernity? These are questions that need to be addressed in the Australian context. Studies in South Asian countries indicate that such differentiation process have already begun in various forms (see, for example, Hussain's and Turner's article in this special issue).

For the sake of the argument of this article let us assume that, as there is work toward an Australian Muslim identity, akin to what is happening in the UK,[50] an Australian *Shari'a*, somewhat above or across ethnic/sectarian Muslim cleavages, might become more systematized somehow. This would fit with the finding that some Islamic social actors are working on Islamic projects of modernity that offer variations from Western thinking.[51] Such religio-social actions should be understood within the multiple modernities thesis. As Göle[52] has explicitly written on this topic within an Islamic context, the multiple-modernities project puts the emphasis on the inclusionary dynamic of modernity, on borrowing, blending, and cross-fertilization, rather than on the logic of exclusionary divergence, binary oppositions (between traditionals and moderns), or the clash of civilizations (between Islam and the West). Göle argues that, within this contemporary phase that explores the boundaries of modernity within an Islamic context, there is a post-Islamic stage in which Islamism is less and less about following political and revolutionary actions, but rather about engaging in social and cultural everyday life practices.[53] "Post-Islamists" would thus be working on new public spaces, on creating their new visibility, lifestyles, and identities. This post-Islamic stage is working so much on redrawing the initial Western project of modernity by bringing Islam into the public space that the author even raises an important question: "The question that needs to be asked is not whether Islam is compatible with modernity but how Islam and modernity interact with each other, transform one another, and reveal each other's limits."[54]

An Australia *Shari'a* would form a component of this post-Islamist project of modernity, but this might not necessarily lead to its acceptance in Australia. The challenge is thus how to have these post-Islamist (from Muslim migrants and their descendants in Australia) and post-Christian (from the creation of Australia as a modern state in 1901) modernities "speak" to each other. In this sense and in this context, the whole challenge of postsecularism is to understand how these two modernities can enter into a dialogue, rather than into a "clash."

However, one should be aware of the difficulties of entering into such a dialogue. Michele Dilon, in her 2009 Association for the Sociology of Religion Presidential Address, stated quite sharply that "independent[ly] of whether an individual is religious or not, tolerance of otherness does not come easily,"[55] that openness to alternative beliefs is more complicated than Habermas might have us believe, and that the idea that all religious and atheist groups can live in a self-reflective manner "is attractive but hard to imagine."[56] The postsecular project is based upon the notion that the state is neutral and objective, and we know in sociology how the state usually and instrumentally serves certain groups over others. Nevertheless, the proposal below may provide, at the least, a further step toward this postsecular project.

TOWARD A MULTIFAITH PRAGMATIC MODERNITY IN AUSTRALIA?

How might we sidestep this possible "clash" of modernities in Australia and move toward a more conducive postsecular dialogue? Curiously, the solution to this problem might be found in the ways that universities, as microcosms of society, deal with religious diversity on their campuses.

Gilliat-Ray created a typology of four different types of universities when dealing with religious matters.[57] The "anti-religious" type makes no provision for religious space, and its statutes forbid the teaching of theology. The "tolerant" type, which is open to religious activity, provides minimum support by way of maintenance to religious spaces. Non-Christian faiths are likely to have to deal with temporary rooms of worship under this model. The "anti-denominational" type provides religious space without this space being the preserve of one faith group alone and ignores differences between faiths. The "multi-faith pragmatist" type of university is the more open and pragmatic type to religious diversity. As Gilliat-Ray comments,

> This is a facility used by all religious groups, but with a separate specially designated area for Muslim prayers. The university interprets secular to mean that special *privilege* should not be accorded to particular religious groups, *while also recognising distinctive needs*, notably of Muslims. It promotes its religious spaces as one aspect of student provision and equal opportunity, and goes beyond neutral tolerance of diversity towards a positive recognition of different religious identities.[58]

Appropriating these ideal types of chaplaincies to the thread of this article, the challenge in Australia would be to move toward what could be called a 'multifaith pragmatic modernity.' By this expression we mean that Australia should have a modernity that is secular in the sense that no special privilege be given to particular religious groups and that, in line with the Family Law Act 1975 (Cth), each group has recognition of their distinctive needs as regards culture and religious law.

However, in reality, one must be aware of the current situation in Australia with regard to its Christian heritage. Randell-Moon[59] and Maddox[60] recently demonstrated that, in the Australian case (a secular liberal society where a strong division between church and state is supposedly definitive), religion has still a part to play in politics. In this "secular" liberal culture where religion is often actually a significant factor in voting decisions and is intruding more and more into the public sphere since the twenty-first century, one should not be surprised to witness the many social and cultural leaks (rather than processes of total de-differentiation) across the spheres of state and religion.

Theories of multiple modernities always link the specific modernity of a nation to its specific history, as if modernity could not move beyond its chain of memory, in Hervieu-Léger's sense. Analyzing this link between Australia's political and religious histories, Chavura[61] states that for the "Fathers of Australian Federation" in 1901, while secularism informed the creation of a new government, this secularism was not nonreligious but nonsectarian. Chavura writes, "Thus, while the Church of England was never established in Federated Australia, there was always space for religious input in matters of social policy, education, welfare, and national ceremony. Australian secularism, like British secularism, has always been open."

In this sense, Australia's current overarching modernity is more nonsectarian than secular (in its contemporary sense), and its history might find a fit with a new multifaith pragmatic project. The problem to solve is that its chain of memory is mainly Christian, and work needs to be done to include non-Christian faiths as well, as nonsectarianism should now be applied to all religions. As there is increasing awareness of the limitations of the Westphalian solution to religious wars, the Hobbesian social contract, and Lockean liberalism as political strategies for managing conflicting religious and ethnic interests,[62] application of a multifaith pragmatic project to legal pluralism might help to progress the debate on *Shari'a* in Western societies, at least with regards to family law.

CONCLUSION: THE CULTURAL TRADITION INHERENT IN AUSTRALIAN LAW AND THE HEGEMONIC EFFECT OF STATE LAW

What are, then, the cultural presuppositions of Australian family law? While Australian family law is often assumed to espouse neutral cultural values, it embraces particular social and moral values such as individual rationality, formal or abstract universalism, the centrality of state justice, and Christian mainstream mores. The present configuration of family law is the outcome of a long historical process that has seen the establishment of a secular state together with the disestablishment of the church and the introduction of the notion that religion should be contained within the private sphere. (The church/secular division is not a clear one, as invariably the state defines the place of religion.[63]) The common law has also evolved through the adaption and acceptance of customary usages.[64]

Several writers have argued that dominant cultures have developed a norm by which minority cultures are acceptable but required to locate their meanings within their own grid.[65] Others, such as Said,[66] have argued that the Western idea of law acts as an exclusionary device, operating to exclude the "other." The ways or means by which dominant cultures exclude meaning for or in minority cultures have been articulated in various fora, but further articulation is needed, at least in the Australian context in relation to exclusion of Muslims from the Australian mainstream.

Recent comments by Australian politicians about *Shari'a* show an uncritical acceptance of conventional wisdoms, such as "equality before the law" and "universality," the incompatibility of pluralism with the rule of law, and the likelihood of "mainstream" legal values to adjust "organically" in response to the cultural diversification of society.[67] We explore the assumptions behind these claims by way of conclusion.

First, these claims rest on the notion that the law will incrementally improve and transform over time as a response to multiculturalism. As James Gobbo, a former Australian judge put it, "[w]e should place our faith in the common law—its deep well—and it will tap the riches of other cultures for all deep wells interconnect'.[68]

Second, the Australian legal system reflects the ideal of universalism: that all should be "equal before the law" and subject to the same code. The claim for universalism is false as it is contingent upon a particular historical evolution and the notion that religion can be contained in the private sphere without violating its historical integrity. This claim may only be made plausible by the assumption of a form of Protestant Christianity that locates the religious essence in a personal and private relationship with God.[69] Our laws do in fact recognize the individual in both a substantive and a formalistic way. The claim of universalism is thus used to bolster conservative claims of authority and position Muslims as problematic and antagonistic.

Third, Australian politicians have claimed that special groups (such as Muslims) should not have particular social advantages. Part of this claim relates to the administrative sphere and concerns who will monitor the decision-making authorities and what standards of interpretations should be applied. This apparently logical claim that the law should be consistent denies the reality that Muslim societies might have, in fact, a system of hybrid law that does not threaten the existing legal system or pose a threat to society.

To progress postsecular dialogues between modernities in Australia, this article recommends that a multifaith pragmatic project be explored in the Australian religious context.

NOTES

1. Marion Boyd, *Dispute Resolution in Family Law: Protecting Choice, Promoting Inclusion* (Ontario: Ministry of the Attorney General, 2004); Rowan Williams, "Civil and Religious Law in England: A Religious Perspective," Archbishop's home page, 2008, http://www.archbishopofcanterbury.org (accessed October 19, 2011).

2. Robert McClelland (Federal Attorney General), "Government Rules out Sharia Law," *Western Australian Newspaper*, February 8, 2008.

3. John Howard, "PM: Costello Comments Right," *Sydney Morning Herald*, February 20, 2006.

4. This erroneous view was promoted in the case of *Refah Partisi (Welfare Party) and Others v. Turkey* (2003) 37 *European Human Rights Reports* 1. For a corrective approach, see Moussa A. Ramadan, "Notes on the Sharia: Human Rights, Democracy and the Human Court of Human Rights," *Israeli Law Review* 40, no. 3 (2007): 156–197.

5. Tariq Ramadan, *Western Muslims and the Future of Islam* (Oxford: Oxford University Press, 2004), 32.

6. Aziz Al-Azmeh, *Islam and Modernities* (London and New York: Verso, 1993), 1.

7. Jurgen Habermas, "Religion in the Public Sphere," *European Journal of Philosophy* 14, no. 1 (2006): 4.

8. Australian Department of Foregin Affairs and Trade, http://www.dfat.gov.au/facts/muslims_in_australia.html (accessed October 17, 2011).

9. Islamic Women's Welfare Council of Victoria, *Race, Faith and Gender: Converging Discriminations Against Muslim Women in Victoria: The Ongoing Impact of September 11* (Melbourne: Islamic Women's Welfare Council of Victoria Inc., 2008).

10. Samina Yasmeen, "Dealing with Islam in Australia: After the London Bombings," *The Sydney Papers* 17, nos. 3/4 (Winter/Spring 2005): 37–42; Samina Yasmeen, "Muslim Women as Citizens in Australia: Diverse Notions and Practices," *Australian Journal of Social Issues* 42, no. 1 (2007): 41–54.

11. Samia Bano, "In Pursuit of Religious and Legal Diversity: A Response to the Archbishop of Canterbury and the 'Sharia Debate' in Britain," *Ecclesiastical Law Journal* 10 (2008): 283–309; Williams, "Civil and Religious Law in England."

12. George Megalogenis, "Howard hits out at 'jihad' Muslims," *The Australian*, February 20, 2006, http://www.theaustralian.news.com.au/story/0,20867,18204301-601,00.html (accessed October 17, 2011).

13. McClelland (2008).

14. John Griffiths, "Legal Pluralism," in *International Encyclopedia of the Social and Behavioral Sciences*, ed. Neil Smelser and Neil J. Baltes (New York: Elsevier, 2001), 8650–654.

15. Australia Law Reform Commission, *The Recognition of Aboriginal Customary Laws*, Report No. 1, AGPS, Canberra, 1986.

16. Government of Western Australia, "Aboriginal Customary Laws, The Interaction of Western Austalian Law with Aboriginal Law and Culture" Project 94, 2006.

17. Ibid.

18. Michael Humphrey, "Community Disputes Violence and Dispute Processing in a Lebanese Muslim Immigrant Community," *Journal of Legal Pluralism* 53 (1984): 21–88.

19. Cf. An-Nai'm Abdullahi, *Islamic Family Law in a Changing World: A Global Resource Book* (London: Zed Books, 2002); John Esposito, *Women in Muslim Family Law* (New York: Syracuse University Press, 1982); Jamal Nasir, *The Islamic Law of Personal Status* (London: Graham & Trotman, 1990).

20. Nina Schiller, "Transborder Citizenship: An Outcome of Legal Pluralism Within Transnational Social Fields," in *Mobile People, Mobile Law: Expanding Legal Relations in a Contracting World*, ed. Franz and Keebet Benda-Beckman (London: Ashgate, 2005).

21. Jamila Hussain, *Islam its Law and Society* (Sydney: Federation Press, 2004), 178–82.

22. David Pearl, "Family Law," in *The Oxford Encyclopedia of the Islamic World*, ed. J. Esposito (Oxford: Oxford University Press, 2001), 461; Maila Stivens, "'Family Values' and Islamic Revival: Gender, Rights and the State in the Moral Projects in Malaysia," *Women's Studies International Forum* 29 (2006): 357.

23. Pearl, "Family Law," 462.

24. Ibid.

25. Edward Said, *Orientalism* (London: Routledge, 1978).

26. Bobby Sayyid, *A Fundamental Fear: Eurocentrism and the Emergence of Islam* (London: Zed Books, 2003), 11.

27. Mohammed Akhtar, *Muslim Family in a Dilemma: Quest for a Western Identity* (Boulder: University Press of America, 2007); Pascale Fournier, "In the (Canadian) Shadow of Islamic Law: Translating Mahr as a Bargaining Endowment," *Osgoode Hall Law Journal* 44, no. 4 (2006): 649–77; Richard Freeland, "The Islamic Institution of Mahr and the American Law," *Gonzaga Journal of International Law* (2000–2001): 1–5; David Pearl and M. Menski, *Muslim Family Law* (London: Sweet and Maxwell, 1998); Ihsan Yilmaz, "Law as Chameleon: The Question of Incorporation of Muslim Personal Law and the English Law," *Journal of Muslim Minority Affairs* 21, no. 2 (2001): 297–308.

28. Australian Broadcasting Corporation (ABC), interview with Damien Carrick, Julie McFarlane, and Haisam Farache, *Law Report*, ABC, October 21, 2008.

29. Ghena Krayem, "Meditation in the Mosque," *ABC National Radio 21*, October 2008.

30. Ibid.

31. Ibid.

32. Samia Bano, "Complexity, Difference and 'Muslim Personal Law': Rethinking the Relationship with Sharia Councils and South Asian Muslim Women" (PhD diss., University of Warwick, 2004), 38.

33. ABC, interview; Denis MacEoin, *Sharia Law or "One Law for All"?* (London: Civitas Institute for the Study of Civil Society, 2009), 4.

34. Ann Black, "Accommodating Shariah Law in Australia's Legal System," *Alternative Law Journal* 33, no. 4 (2008): 214–19; Pearl and Menski, *Muslim Family Law*, 57.

35. Will Kymlicka, *Liberalism, Community and Culture* (New York: Clarendon Press, 1989); Iris Marion Young, *Justice and the Politics of Difference* (Princeton: Princeton University Press, 1990).

36. Gordan Woodman, "Legal Pluralism and the Search for Justice," *Journal of African Law* 40, no. 2 (1996): 152–67.

37. Bryan S. Turner, "Religious Authority and the New Media," *Theory, Culture & Society* 24, no. 2 (2007): 117–34.

38. Jose Casanova, "Rethinking Secularization: A Global Comparative Perspective," *The Hedgehog Review* 8, nos. 1/2 (2006): 7–22; Grace Davie, "Is Europe an Exceptional Case?," *The Hedgehog Review* 8, nos. 1/2 (2006): 23–34; David Martin, *On Secularization: Towards a Revised General Theory* (Ashgate: Aldershot, 2005).

39. Shmuel N. Eisenstadt, "Multiple Modernities," *Daedalus* 129, no. 1 (2000): 2.

40. Casanova, "Rethinking Secularization."

41. Davie, "Is Europe an Exceptional Case?"

42. Grace Davie, *Europe: The Exceptional Case. Parameters of Faith in the Modern World* (London: Darton, Longman and Todd, 2002).

43. Ibid., 147–50.

44. Adam Possamai, "Australia's 'Shy' De-secularisation Process," in *Religion, Spirituality & Social Science*, ed. Alia Imtoual and Basia Spalek (Bristol: Policy Press, 2008): 23–35.

45. Adam Possamai and Alphia Possamai-Inesedy, "The Baha'i Faith and Caodaism: Migration, Change and De-secularisation(s) in Australia," *Journal of Sociology* 43, no. 3 (2007): 301–18; Possamai, "Australia's 'Shy' De-secularisation Process"; Deborah Stevenson et al., "Sydney: An Examination of a 'Post-Secular' World City," *Australian Geographer* 41, no. 3 (2010): 323–50.

46. Gary Bouma, *Australian Soul: Religion and Spirituality in the Twenty-first Century* (Cambridge: Cambridge University Press, 2006).

47. Ibid., 2.

48. Ibid.

49. Volker Schmidt, "One World, One Modernity," in *Modernity at the Beginning of the 21st Century*, ed. Volker H. Schmidt (Newcastle: Cambridge Scholars Publishing, 2007), 205–28.

50. Hisham A. Hellyer, "British Muslims: Past, Present and Future," *The Muslim World* 97 (2007): 249.

51. Adam Possamai, *Sociology of Religion for Generations X and Y* (London: Equinox, 2009).

52. Nilufer Göle, "Snapshots of Islamic Modernities," *Daedalus* 129, no. 1 (2000): 91–117.

53. Göle (2000), 94.

54. Göle (2000), 94.

55. Michele Dillon, "2009 Association for the Sociology of Religion Presidential Address. Can Post-Secular Society Tolerate Religious Differences?," *Sociology of Religion* 71, no. 2 (2010): 149.

56. Ibid.,152.

57. Sophie Gilliat-Ray, *Religion in Higher Education: The Politics of the Multi-faith Campus* (Ashgate: Aldershot, 2000).

58. Ibid., 97.

59. Holly Randell-Moon, "Tolerating Religious 'Others': Some Thoughts on Secular Neutrality and Religious Tolerance in Australia," *The Australian Religion Studies Review* 22, no. 3 (2009): 324–44.

60. Marion Maddox, "An Argument for More, Not Less, Religion in Australian Politics," *The Australian Religion Studies Review* 22, no. 3 (2009): 345–67.

61. Stephen Chavura, "The Secularization Thesis and the Secular State: Reflections with Special Attention to Debates in Australia," in *Religion and the State: From Deprivatisation To Securitization, And From Pietism To Consumerism*, ed. Jack Barbalet, Adam Possamai, and Bryan Turner (New York: Anthem Press, forthcoming).

62. Jack Barbalet, Adam Possamai, and Bryan Turner, eds., "Religion and the State in Pluralistic Environments," *Australian Religion Studies Review* Special Issue, (forthcoming).

63. Talal Asad, *Formations of the Secular: Christianity, Islam Modernity* (Stanford: Stanford University Press, 2003); Sophie Sunderland, "Post Secular Nation; or How Australian Spirituality Privileges a Secular, White Judaeo-Christian Culture," *Transforming Cultures* 2, no. 1 (2007): 57–77; Tom Frame, *Church and State: Australians Imaginary Wall* (Sydney: UNSW Press, 2006).

64. Harry W. Arthurs,*"Without the Law": Administrative Justice and Legal Pluralism in Nineteenth- Century England* (Toronto: University of Toronto Press, 1985).

65. Homi Bhabha, "The Third Space," in *Identity, Community, Culture, Difference*, ed. J. Rutherford (London: Lawrence and Wishart, 1990), 208.

66. Said, *Orientalism*.

67. Luke McNamara, "Equality Before the Law in Polyethnic Societies: The Construction of Normative Criminal Law Standards," *Murdoch Electronic Law Journal* (2004), http://www.murdoch.edu.au/elaw/issues/v11n2/mcnamara112.html (accessed October 17, 2011).

68. James Gobbo, *Law in a Multicultural Society* (Canberra: Australian Institute of Multicultural Affairs, 1983), 6.

69. Daniel Celermajer, "If Islam is Our Other, Who are 'We,'" *Australian Journal of Social Issues* 47, no. 1 (2007): 112.

A Dual Legal System in Australia: The Formalization of *Shari'a*

Jan A. Ali

School of Humanities and Languages, University of Western Sydney, Australia

Legal pluralism, or the dual legal system, is in essence a postcolonial phenomenon. People movement—migration—from the poor South to the rich North started in earnest at the end of the colonial era. Many Muslims were part of this migration process, and as a result we have today a visible Muslim presence in many countries of the West. In a number of Western countries, demand by Muslims for dual legal system is fast growing and is a direct legacy of postcolonial migration processes. Great Britain, for example, which has over two million Muslims, in late 2008 officially endorsed *Shari'a* (Islamic law) tribunals governing marriage, divorce, and inheritance to make legally binding decisions when parties involved agree. This article looks at the Muslim call for the dual legal system in Australia in relation to the establishment of *Shari'a* as a separate code of law and explores the basis upon which such a call rests. It argues that this demand by Muslims in Australia is not only premature but sociologically unsustainable. Although Islam is a permanent feature of Australian multiculturalism and the Muslim population through migration and birth is fast increasing, Muslims in Australia remain divided on ethnic, parochial, and ideological lines. To gather this fragmentary community to any religious function is enormously difficult, let alone getting it to agree on a set of Islamic legal codes or the *Shari'a*.

INTRODUCTION

A dual legal system is in essence a postcolonial phenomenon. People movement—migration—from a poor South to a rich North started in earnest at the end of the colonial era in the 1970s. Many Muslims were part of this migration process, and as a result we have today a visible Muslim presence in many countries of the West, including Australia.

In a number of Western countries today, demand by Muslims for the establishment of a dual legal system through the formalization of *Shari'a* (Islamic law) is fast growing and is a direct legacy of postcolonial migration processes. Great Britain, for example, which has over two million Muslims, in late 2008 officially endorsed *Shari'a* tribunals governing marriage, divorce, and inheritance to make legally binding decisions when parties involved agree.

This article looks at the issue of a dual legal system in Australia in relation to the formalization of *Shari'a* and its juxtapositioning as a separate code of law from Australia's civil legal system. It explores the existence of a potential need for the formalization of *Shari'a*. Islam is a permanent feature of Australian multiculturalism, wherein the Muslim population through migration, birth, and conversion is exponentially increasing, along with Muslim piety and the awareness and implementation of *Shari'a*. However, Muslim social and religious experiences do not support this demand in any coherent way, and the Australian Muslim explanation for the need to formalize *Shari'a* is not analytically convincing. In this article I want to argue that a Muslim call for the establishment of a dual legal system through the formalization of *Shari'a* in Australia is not only premature but sociologically unsustainable. Given that Muslims in Australia constitute only 1.7 percent of the total Australian population, which is ethnically, parochially, and ideologically diverse and divided, and also given that a vast majority of Muslims only selectively practice their faith while many do not practice at all, any agreement of Australian Muslims on one set of laws and order is a sociologically challenging goal and requires first the development of a coherent religious community before *Shari'a* can be considered for formalization in Australia.

SHARI'A

Shari'a (Islamic law), literally meaning "the path leading to the watering place," is the fundamental religious concept of Islam and the essence of Muslim faith. It is used in the Qur'ān in relation to a way toward or purpose of faith (Sūra 45: 18).[1] *Shari'a* is used in relation to the whole system of law and jurisprudence within the religion of Islam. The principal Islamic ethos demands Muslims to surrender to the Will of Allah in totality, and Allah's command for Muslim *ummah* is expressed through the *Shari'a* and constitutes a system of duties that all faithful believers must fulfill.

For Muslims, *Shari'a* is founded on the words of Allah as revealed in the Qur'ān and the *hadith*—reports of the sayings of the Prophet Muhammad. The Qur'ānic revelations laid down basic standards of conduct upon which the Prophet Muhammad established his first *ummah* (Muslim community).

The Qur'ān provides a variety of ethico-legal teachings. Some of these have a universal application while others are specific to particular circumstances and material conditions. Faruqi tells us that

> . . . .Muslims have recognized the imperatives and desiderata of the Qur'an as falling into different orders of rank or priority. Although they all belong to the divine will and are constitutive of it, Qur'anic values do not all enjoy the same degree of normativeness. Some are more fundamental and important than others. Some are direct and specific in what they demand of man; some are indirect, pointing to general directions. Some are explicit and comprehensible on first reading; others are implicit and have to be deduced from one or more Qur'anic premises.[2]

The Qur'ān no doubt presents the key elements of legislation and contains legal instructions. As Hallaq explains,

> The traditional count of all legal verses comes to about five hundred—a number that at first glance seems exiguous, considering the overall size of the Quran. . . . these verses represent a larger weight than the number may indicate. It is common knowledge that the Quran repeats itself both literally and thematically, but this tendency of repetition is absent in the legal subject matter. The proportion of the legal verses, therefore, is larger than that suggested by an absolute number. And if we consider the fact that the average length of the legal verses is twice or even thrice that of the non-legal verses, it is not difficult to argue. . . . that the Quran contains no less legal material than does the Torah. . . .[3]

Muslims believe that *Shari'a* is by nature a text-based law originating from the sacred sources of Islam: the Qur'ān as the literal word of Allah and *hadith* as the tradition—words and deeds—of Muhammad the Prophet. Apart from these two primary sacred sources that constitute the basis of *Shari'a*, there are three other secondary sources: *ijma* (scholarly consensus), *qiyas* (reasoning by analogy), and *ijtihad* (individual reasoning, which is an intellectual property for increasing *ilm* (knowledge of traditional practice and the trained capacity to deduce from it, using *ray* or juristic opinion). Combined, these five sources form the complete basis of *Shari'a*.

When it comes to the question of how Muslims should follow the *Shari'a*, scholars traditionally have developed five categories into which the Qur'ān's ethico-legal teachings fall. In Islamic law, the entire array of human actions falls into one of the five categories. These are as follows:

1. Obligatory (for example, five pillars of Islam),
2. Prohibited (for example, consumption of alcohol),
3. Recommended (for example, marriage),
4. Reprehensible (for example, divorce), and
5. Permissible (for example, polygamy).

Unlike understandings of law in the secular modern context or in the Western sense, *Shari'a* is much more than law. This is because it not only covers dogma, rituals, ethics, and morality, but also deals with "purity" concerning ritual washing and bodily functions and, further, includes laws relating to civil, commercial, criminal, administrative, and other matters. Mohammad Kamali says that *Shari'a* relates not only to a "code of law" but to religion as a way of life—*din*—based on the idea of the unity of God, prayer, charity, fasting, and pilgrimage. He contends that the fundamental focus of the *Shari'a* is the five pillars of Islam. Moreover, *Shari'a* also pays heed to the defense of life, religion, offspring, dignity, and intellect; prevention of injustice and promotion of justice; and prevention of social ill and promotion of social benefit.[4]

Malise Ruthven says that

> By common consent the Shari'a or holy law represents the greatest historic achievement of Islam as a religious cultural system, providing Muslim societies with a degree of order and authority under the "rule of God" that counterbalanced the instability that often prevailed at the political level.[5]

The *Shari'a* is then a corpus of rules of divine origin implemented by human agency to govern private worship and social relations. It specifies the rules and regulations governing the lives of the faithful believers. It is a way of life, a "complete exchange," in which all important religious, legal, moral, ethical, social, cultural, economic, and political institutions find simultaneous expression. From a Weberian perspective, it exhibits a "substantive rationality" within which morality, ethics, law, religion, economy, and politics are enmeshed, in contrast to a "formal rationality" (which Weber associates exclusively with Western capitalism), within which law is separate from other parts of societal structure and operates under its distinct code of conduct and conventions. Izzi Dien sheds further light on the construction and concept of *Shari'a,* arguing that it

> covers all aspects of human existence, including life after death. It does not represent a set of theories and rules to be utilised within the limits of social government, but signifies a comprehensive way of life, which is similar to a path leading to water, as the word *Shari'a* implies. The law is inextricably bound with the faith, following its route and regulating its orders and directives.[6]

Shari'a constitutes a code of behavior divinely decreed to guide the believer in his or her literal execution of religious duties in this world and quest for divine favor in the Hereafter. Due to the centrality of *Shari'a* in Islam since its systematization during the second and third Islamic centuries, it has remained pivotal in the mainstream discourses and institutions of Muslim societies.

Shari'a is better understood with the help of an Islamic jurisprudential tool known as *fiqh*. *Fiqh*, which literally means "understanding" or "knowledge," is Islamic jurisprudence used to define rules and methodologies of law. It is the methodology employed to work out and apply the law. *Fiqh* is a jurisprudential corpus mainly produced in the second and third centuries of Islam by the *ulama* or private scholars, with unique methods of reasoning and argument.[7] It effectively became the corpus of the *Shari'a* as developed from the canonical sources and implemented to address issues facing Muslims relating to their practices of worship and social relationships. In essence then, *fiqh* is a science of ascertaining a wholesome understanding of *Shari'a* and is a discipline that permits academic discussion and exegetical analysis of Islamic practice.

In the *fiqh* study of the classical form of *Shari'a*, Islamic law is clearly different from Western systems of law in two distinct ways. First, *Shari'a*, as I mentioned above, unlike most other legal systems, covers all personal and public aspects of everyday life including regulation of the individual's relationship with God. *Shari'a* governs ethical standards as well as legal rules, demonstrating clearly what individuals are permitted to do as well as, in conscience, prohibited to do. Second, *Shari'a* differs from Western legal systems in that it gives expression to Divine Will, which ceased in terms of divine revelation with the death of Prophet Muhammad. As totally distinct from the secular legal system or civil law that evolves from/in secular societies and changes in light of the changing material conditions of people, *Shari'a* was forced upon Islamic society from above through the institution of caliphate. In secular modern contexts, or in Western legal systems, law is made by humans who have the authority and power to legislate. However, in Islam the *fiqh* decrees that the role of the society's members, as vicegerents, is not to create legislation but merely to implement it.

The foundation of Islamic law, which was originally laid down by the Prophet, was expanded upon by the orthodox companions. As Islam grew and expanded politically and militarily, the law of Islam gradually spread throughout the Muslim world. Inevitably, from this legal system grew some individual interpretations, which in turn brought forth scholarly polemics regarding a host of legal cases. Eventually, two fundamental legal methodological viewpoints emerged concerning the process of understanding the law. One viewpoint would focus on the texts alone and the other would point to individual reasoning to supplement the texts when delivering an injunction.

In reaction to the emergence of the two legal methodological viewpoints and the crisis of Umayyad (661–750) and Abbasid (750–1258) dynasties, four Sunni jurisprudential schools emerged in second Islamic century. The four schools were Ḥanafite, Mālikite, Shāfi'ite and Ḥanbalite, named respectively by their putative founders Abū Ḥanīfa, Mālik ibn Anas, Ash-Shāfi'ī, and Aḥmad ibn Ḥanbal. With the development of different schools of law, by the middle of the second Islamic century the law had become more comprehensive in coverage (although it would take another fifty years to develop fully), and jurists had started to develop their own legal reasoning and methodologies.[8]

There exists a variety of explanatory models that seek to shed light on the formation of the *Shari'a*. However, it needs to be appreciated that this legislative development began within the Qur'ān itself and the Prophet's blueprints of a future life pattern for Muslims, drawn up under varying conditions of Islam in Mecca and Medina and shaping a cultural trajectory that has persisted for over fourteen hundred years and has produced, in its continuance, a wide range of legal cultures. Equally important to remember is the fact that "the law" was the direct result of the analytical study of the vibrant, great texts of Islam (Qur'ān and *hadiths*) that undoubtedly had a mammoth impact on Muslim legal life. The interpretive relationship between the *ulama* and jurists, and the Qur'ān and *hadiths*, was analogous to the relationship between the Divine text—Qur'ān—and the Sunna during the Prophetic career of Muhammad. However, the correlation could not be sustained forever because new situations and Islam's entry into new cultural systems required corresponding legislation, implemented in light of the Divine text and the Prophet's articulation of *maslaha mursala*. The Prophet set out the principles and methods of using the Qur'ānic teaching to address issues emerging in society. These proved to be important guidelines for the *ulama* and jurists, who used them to interpret the texts to suit the demands of their everyday living.

Having discussed rather briefly the fundamental elements of Islamic law and jurisprudence, let us now turn our focus to Australian Muslims and assess the prospect for utility and application of Islamic law. Let's begin by looking at the process of Muslim migration, its impact on the evolution of Islam in Australia, and consequential implications for the *Shari'a*.

MUSLIM MIGRATION

Muslims started to arrive in Australia in greater numbers in 1970s and 1980s, and the last quarter of the twentieth century saw a steep increase in the growth of Australia's Muslim population. Thus in 1991 there were 148,096 Muslims who constituted 0.9 percent of the total Australian population; in 1996 there were 200,902 Muslims making up 1.1 percent; in 2001, 281,578 reaching 1.5 percent; and by 2006, 340,389 Muslims constituting 1.7 percent.[9] Though Muslims live in many areas across the Australian continent, they are mainly concentrated in the states of New South Wales and Victoria (as Table 1 below shows), and mainly live in the states' capital cities.[10] In New South Wales, where the largest Muslim population lives, Muslim Australians constituted 2.5 percent of the total state population in 2006. Within New South Wales, over 50 percent of the Muslim population reside almost entirely within a radius of 50 kilometres of Sydney, making Sydney the site for the most concentrated Muslim population in Australia.[11]

Table 1: Australian Muslim population by state/territory.

Census year	2001	2006
New South Wales	140, 907	168, 786
Victoria	92, 742	109, 370
Western Australia	19, 456	24, 186
Queensland	14, 990	20, 321
South Australia	7, 478	10, 517
Australian Capital Territory	3, 488	4, 373
Northern Territory	945	1, 089
Tasmania	865	1, 050
Other Territories	707	700
Total	281, 578	340, 392

Note. Source: Australian Bureau of Statistics (ABS) 2001 and 2006 Censuses of Population and Housing.

Table 2: Top 10 countries of birth.

Country	Percent
Australia	37.9
Lebanon	8.9
Turkey	6.8
Afghanistan	4.7
Pakistan	4.1
Bangladesh	3.9
Iraq	2.9
Indonesia	2.5
Bosnia and Herzegovina	2.2
Iran	2.1
Other	24.0

Note. Source: Australian Bureau of Statistics (ABS) 2006 Census of Population and Housing.

This steady, yet rapid, increase in the Muslim population has been mainly attributed to immigration, although high birth rates have also contributed. Table 2 below shows that the Muslim birth rate in Australia is a significant factor in Muslim population growth. If this trend continues, it is possible that second and third generation Muslims could gradually expand the Muslim population over the years and that Islam would then become an important factor in Australia's social, economic, and political reality.

Muslims, in most parts of the world, are not a homogeneous people and are divided essentially on sectarian and ethnic grounds. Australia's Muslim population is also very diverse, and Table 2 above provides a glimpse into this diversity. According to Saeed,[12] Sunnis make up the majority Muslims in Australia, followed by the various *Shī'ah* sects such as *Zaidīyah*, *Ismāīliyya*, *Druze*, *Ja'farī yah*, and *'Ālawīyah*. There are traces of *Aḥmadism* (a Muslim sect founded by a Muslim scholar known as Mirzā Ghūlām Aḥmad in 1901 in India) and *Wahḥābism* (a Muslim revivalist movement founded by 'Abdūl Wahḥāb in Saudi Arabia), as well as of various other minor sects. Between 1975 and 2000, Muslims have come from over seventy different nations, and this makes Muslims ethnically the most diverse religious group in Australia.[13]

MUSLIM ETHNIC IDENTITY

Like migrants in general, Muslims migrated to Australia for various reasons. Economic advantages and educational opportunities, family reunion, and escaping political oppression in their homelands are some of the more prominent rationales for Muslims making Australia their permanent home.[14] While some migrants came from Islamic monocultures such as Afghanistan, Pakistan, and Syria, a lot of them arrived from countries like Albania, Lebanon, and Nigeria, which are themselves culturally and religiously diverse.[15] As a result, Muslim migrants have different experiences of Australian society, and these cannot be homogenized. The plurality of Muslims and their experience as migrants contrasts strongly with the popular media representations of Islam and Muslims being uniform and homogeneous.

The majority of these migrants settled in large capital cities, particularly Sydney and Melbourne.[16] The overwhelming concentration of Muslim immigrants in these two capital cities corresponded to the settlement patterns of Mediterranean migrants. In the case of Muslim immigrants, 50 percent settled in Sydney and 23 percent in Melbourne, according to 1991 Australian Census.[17] These large urban centers provided relatively cheap accommodation, particularly in their outer suburbs, and offered employment in the manufacturing and service industries. They were also homes to other groups from the same ethnic backgrounds, which met the sociocultural and emotional needs of new Muslim immigrants.[18] Thus, Muslim immigrants settled close to each other. Following the dominant pattern of immigrant settlement in Australia, they gravitated toward their own ethnic circles and concentrated in the working class suburbs of Sydney and Melbourne.[19] In Sydney, for instance, Muslim communities are concentrated in the four Local Government Areas of Bankstown, Canterbury, Auburn, and Liverpool.[20] Humphrey observes that chain migration—by which individuals immigrated and later brought over families, relatives, and friends—and close settlement were pivotal in creating the geographical concentration of Muslim immigrants, a situations that emphasizes the significance of social relations based on parochial and family ties and ethnicity.[21] Humphrey claims that "Muslim immigrants have entered Australian society through the cultural mediums of family, community and religion which have located them in social spaces shaping their status, employment and residence patterns."[22]

According to Humphrey this has meant that the established social relations of the family and village community have become even more firm and indispensable resources of social exchange in themselves,[23] as distinct from Islam in general or its essence, the *Shari'a*. Consequently, these relations have helped create social microcosms. These social microcosms have been meticulously built through the application of personal efforts in homemaking, family creation, and ethnic language maintenance.

It is not Islam and its essence the *Shari'a* but family and community bonds that have been of paramount importance for Muslim immigrants, for whom the bonds have been a source of support during settlement and a means of reestablishing their traditional social worlds and, ultimately, obtaining Australian citizenship. Family, in particular, has been the principal resource in reproducing social and religious culture. Chain migration made immigration possible and acted as the vehicle for penetrating the broader society. Family and community bonds facilitated residential grouping from which emerged Muslim community and religious life. As Humphrey notes, "[t]he family and village community was used as the basis for recreating community and re-establishing religious life."[24]

Though Islamic institutions such as family and communal relationships were very important for fostering social values and relations, they nonetheless were embedded in ethnicity and parochialism and not in Islam, especially not in what may be described as pristine or scriptural Islam. Ethnic and parochial Islam was the religion many Muslims practiced. Thus, when Muslims first arrived in greater numbers as migrants in 1970s and 1980s, Islam developed as a migrant culture manifesting ethnic and parochial values and traditions in religious practices, rituals, and community organizations. Muslim religious practices and rituals closely resembled ethnic and parochial values and constituted a Muslim culture that was in many respects divorced from scriptural Islam, and its connection with *Shari'a* was weak and fragmentary. Marriage, divorce, and inheritance were managed by village community organizations and in many instances by individuals themselves who accessed Australian secular institutions responsible for the management of such affairs. In the literature about first-generation Muslims in Australia, *Shari'a* is a scantly discussed topic, and one wonders about its importance and implementation in everyday living of these Muslims. Although Muslim religious life has gone through a sharp change in the last decade under the process of Islamic revivalism (a point I shall revisit later in my article), prior to this period it was very much pursued along ethnic and parochial lines, and many key Islamic tenets and rituals were selectively observed and in many cases even ignored.

MUSLIM COMMUNITIES AND ISLAMIC ORGANIZATIONS

Family and village communities formed the original basis for the Muslim community and the reestablishment of Muslim life in Australia. Muslim organizations, in many cases, emerged from the activities of village community organizations. Humphrey asserts that these Muslim community organizations have been the product of family and community ties.[25] He argues that Muslim immigrant community religious life was one aspect of village community activities, and that as the community grew, so did the community's needs. This made necessary the establishment of a separate institution that could cater to multiple aspects of Muslim community life.[26] For example, village social centers or community meeting places frequently developed into provisional prayer halls and subsequently, as the population grew and demand increased, into mosques. Muslim immigrant cultures and practices emerged from these localized sets of contacts in multicultural Australia. Muslim village associations, rather than Islamic institutions, were important bodies for community life and played a key role in the process of settlement.[27]

Islam was not pursued as a way of life and did not constitute a "complete exchange." The key religious, moral, ethical, legal, social, cultural, economic, and political institutions did not find simultaneous expression in the everyday living of Muslim immigrants. Muslims, having their attention focused on the material pursuits of life, paid very little, if any, attention to the central role played by *Shari'a* in Islam. The key religious interest for first-generation Muslims was the arrangement of what may be described within the local Muslim community framework as Muslim life-cycle rituals (which were themselves intimately rooted in ethnicity and not in religion "proper"): birth, marriage, and death.

To look after the affairs of Muslims in Australia, various organizations or "Islamic societies" came into existence. There are many small associations from different countries such as India, Pakistan, Afghanistan, Bangladesh, Malaysia, Indonesia, Fiji, South Africa, Yugoslavia, Bosnia, Albania, and numerous Middle Eastern states, although the two largest Muslim associations were founded by Turkish and Lebanese Muslims. Ordinarily, individual associations have opted for the maintenance of separate identities rather than being ruled by a single national body. Muslim associations and mosques have emerged from specific communities, and ethnic pride has always played a divisive role, causing and effectively rendering Muslims in Australia a heterogeneous community.[28]

Muslim immigrants started establishing Islamic societies as early as the 1950s. The Islamic Society of New South Wales in Sydney, for instance, was set up in 1957. Then, in 1960, the Lebanese Muslim Association of Sydney came into being. The Islamic Society of Victoria in Melbourne and similar societies in Adelaide, Perth, and Brisbane were all founded in 1962. In 1973, the

Islamic Council of New South Wales was formed, in spite of the existence of a national Islamic body, the Australian Federation of Islamic Societies (AFIS), which was formed in 1964. The Australian Federation of Islamic Societies was restructured in 1976 into a three-tiered system comprising local societies, state councils, and a national federation.[29] During this restructuring, the organization changed its name to the Australian Federation of Islamic Councils (AFIC), and the headquarters was moved from Melbourne to Zetland, an inner-city suburb of Sydney, where it has since remained.

In the beginning, the interests and activities of AFIC were not firmly linked to broader Islamic practices and arrangements within the local societies. It was, in fact, at the time more firmly focused on the certification of *ḥalāl* (permissible) meat, particularly for export to Muslim countries in the Middle East. Subsequently, with financial backing from the Saudi Arabian Government, AFIC grew steadily both in its structure and activities.[30] A new Muslim school was established in the western Sydney suburb of Chullora, closer links were forged with local societies and Islamic councils, and more societies and Islamic Councils were established in states and suburbs where the demand existed.

Currently, the three-tiered organizational structure of AFIC remains firmly in existence. But even though its national and international profile has grown over the years, as has its influence over the Muslim community, there are always various groups pressuring for improvement. Potentially, AFIC could attempt to exercise even greater influence over Muslims in Australia, particularly in terms of overcoming the many barriers that divide Muslim ethnic communities. Given this potential, Islamic cultural and organizational structures—particularly the role of the family and community in the process of enculturation—need to be understood in the context of immigrant culture.

Having said this, it is important to note that a number of Muslim organizations, mosques communities, and groups influence intercommunity discourses in Australia. These include sympathizers with international Islamic movements such as the *Al-Ikhwān al-Muslimūn* (Muslim Brotherhood) that have immigrated to Australia. One such group in Australia is the *Ahl al-Sunnah wā'al-Jamā'at Association*, based in the outer Sydney suburb of Lakemba, which describes itself as part of the "global Islamic movement." Other movements that were established outside of Australia but have Australian sympathizers include the *Tablīgh Jamā'at* (Convey [message of Islām] Group), *Jamā'at-i Islāmī* (Islamic Association), and *Ḥizb al-Taḥrīr* (Liberation Party). Although differences exist in the articulation of Islamic doctrine among these movements, they all developed as part of Islamic revivalism during the European colonial period of the Muslim world. What all these movements stress is the need to preserve the individual Muslim character and the unity of the *ummah* (Muslim community). Hence, they naturally find a place in the functions of mosques, schools, youth groups, and other community activities.

ISLAMIC REVIVALISM AND SECOND-GENERATION MUSLIMS

Gary Bouma et al. argue that, as elsewhere, there is a phenomenon of Islamic revivalism emerging in Australia, within which Muslim immigrants are showing signs of increased religiosity:

> The experience of migration and rearing children in [an Australian] socio-religious environment, as well as being in a minority group, has enhanced the religiosity of some [Muslims]. Believing and practising a minority religion, [Muslims] are forced to rediscover who they are and how they are to live."[31]

Bouma et al. believe that a number of factors are responsible for the increase in religiosity in Muslims in Australia. For some Muslim immigrants, conformity to Islam provides a sense of security and protects them from "alien intrusions"—the penetration of foreign values and practices. For others, holding tenaciously to Islamic values and practices offers feelings of satisfaction and tranquillity during periods of personal or social crisis and transition: "Some Muslim migrants intensified their religious practice in their new society for fear of losing their own religiosity and to socialize their children in the family's religion. [Further still, some]. . . . did this to present good role models for their children."[32] This increase in conformity to Islam has become quite common among Australian Muslims today. Even among Muslim youth there is evidence of Islamic revivalism. Evidence of Islamic revivalism can also be seen, for instance, in some Muslim women wearing *ḥijāb* (veil) or *burq'ah* (ladies outer garment covering the whole body) to work, universities, shopping centers, and other public places; in some Muslim men sporting beards and wearing Muslim *kameez* (long baggy shirt) and *shalwar* (baggy trousers) or an Arab-style gown known as *jubb'ah* (flowing Arab robe) in public places; and in provisions for prayer being sought in some workplaces and universities.

Tariq Ramadan has argued in *Islam and Muslims in Europe: A Silent Revolution Toward Rediscovery* (2002) that second and third generation European-born Muslims have helped reorient the political debate from the temporariness of the Muslim presence in Europe to their permanency.[33] He claims that many Muslims at the moment do not

> have a genuine feeling of belonging within the European society. The mindset that prevails among some second- and third-generation Muslims that one should live isolated, ignoring the societal context without even having mastered the language, makes no sense. The community is the place for enlightenment of the spirit and should provide serenity and an intellectual vigour that permit the blossoming of the Muslim individual as a European citizen.[34]

Thus, Ramadan argues, Muslims have been living in Europe for a substantial time and the raising of the issue of a permanent Muslim presence in Europe by second- and third-generation Muslims is a serious attempt on their part "to carve a place for themselves within European intellectual and social spheres."[35] For second- and third-generation Muslims Europe is not a *dār al-ḥarb* (abode of war or un-Islam) as it was once seen by their immigrant parents, but "home," a *dār al-Islām* (abode of Islam) "where Muslims. . . . [should be permitted] to live in security and according to [Islamic] law."[36] Thus, unlike first-generation immigrants, these younger Muslims demand (with the strength of their European citizenship) the right to express their faith visibly and develop a truly European Islamic culture.

As is the case in Europe, in Australia second-generation Muslims are becoming increasingly involved with Islam through participating in what Lars Pedersen refers to as "newer Islamic Movements."[37] These are movements of nonethnic tendencies with a focus on making Muslims better Muslims, based on the Islamic scripture. Nonethnic or universalistic revivalist movements such as the *Jamā'at Da'wah Islāmiah* and the *Tablīgh Jamā'at* in Australia fall into the category of "newer Islāmic movements." These two movements are nonpolitical, ascetic, and de-ethnicized movements engaged in proselytization. In Australia they appeal to *Sunni* Muslims[38] from all walks of life, including a large section of Muslim youths. Muslim youths, who are second-generation Australians, are particularly attracted to the *Tablīgh Jamā'at* as they increasingly deal with a series of challenges on a number of fronts such as racial discrimination, high unemployment, rising "Islamophobia," and intergenerational tension.

DISCUSSION AND CONCLUSION

The existence of the need for a dual legal system through the formalization of the *Shari'a* in Australia may have multiple bases; however, I want to argue here that "Islamization of Muslim life" has always featured as the most prominent basis which, therefore, deserves to be prioritized in discussion. Both internationally and in Australia, there has been a growing trend toward Islamization of Muslim life in the last three decades. It is a post-colonial trend deeply embedded in a global phenomenon known as Islamic revivalism. Islamization of Muslim life, or Islamic revivalism more broadly, is a response to the crisis of modernity (rising unemployment, inequality, and poverty; increase in prejudices, discrimination, and injustices; decline in education, social welfare, and political stability), and is occurring through a process of proselytization whereby increasing number of Muslims are learning new Islamic knowledge, becoming more aware of their religious obligations, and adopting Islamic teachings in a variety of facets of everyday living. A growing number of mosques, prayer halls, Muslims businesses, Muslim schools, educational centers, after-hours Islamic classes under certain sheikhs, and Arabic classes for young and adult Muslims, have emerged and impacted upon Islamic identity and practice under the rubric of Islamic revivalism. Many

Muslims who were previously partial to *Shari'a,* or who pursued a life in which observance of *Shari'a* was absent or minimal, are now observing *Shari'a* in their everyday life with increased vigilance, austerity, rigour and consistency. My own research into the *Tablīgh Jamā'at* in Australia clearly demonstrates this.[39]

The *Tablīgh Jamā'at* are largely second-generation Muslims (some migrant Muslims are also involved), many of whom have opted for a serious religious life (offering regular prayers, engaging in remembrance of God, participating in preaching tours and missions, marrying young and starting family early, and generally observing religious tenets consistently and seriously). Others, after experimenting with a liberal lifestyle punctuated with sexual promiscuity, consumption of drugs and alcohol, indulging in music and discotheque, clubbing, gambling, eating *haram* (not permissible), and so forth have adopted for a serious "Islamic way of life" in many important respects. They now eat *halal* food, dress in Muslim or Islamic attire, offer ritual daily prayers, visit mosques regularly, and have taken a journey to Makka to perform Hajj. Many aspects of their religious life are *Shari'a*-based, and unlike the majority of the previous generation of Muslims their lives are largely shaped and governed by the tenets of scriptural Islam or de-ethnicized and de-parochialized religious culture. Their identity is rooted in religion proper and they project an Islam whose essence is largely the scripture and not ethnic and parochial values. There is a *Shari'a*-based scriptural Islam. Of course, within this camp a universal or homogeneous trend in religious rituals and practices is absent, but a vast majority of this group of Muslims follow very strict religious rules and regulations.

It is largely these strict Muslims who demand, with the authority and power of their citizenship, the establishment of a dual legal system through the formalization of *Shari'a*. They are fluent in the official language of Australia, have a sound education, and have a much better understanding and even experience of the operational functions of key institutions in society. The premise of their claim is that to live a proper life as a Muslim one has to adhere to God's orders, and this can only be possible with God's rules governing personal affairs as well as social relationships and exchanges. They argue that Islam is a religious system revealed by God for the entirety of humanity and for all time. In this way it covers all facets of the life of the individual, society, and caliphate. The *Shari'a*, according to them, is a Divine Law given by God and is, therefore, the most ideal set of directives for human conduct.

They believe that, since Australia is a liberal democracy and they are the citizens of Australia, they have the right to practice their religion freely—a religion whose essence is the Divine Law—*Shari'a*. Formalization of *Shari'a* or their demand for formalization of *Shari'a* is a mere exercise of their citizenship rights in a liberal democracy. A demand, if successful, will enable them to lead what they perceive to be a true Islamic way of life.

However, the formalization of *Shari'a* would mean that Australia would have a dual legal system. In principle, this is not necessarily impractical or unachievable; the situations in Malaysia and Indonesia testify to this. However, as I mentioned above, *Shari'a* differs from Western systems of law in two important ways. My concern is manifold. First, given the fact that *Shari'a* governs all aspects of life and is a complete legal system that permeates entire lives, its partial implementation, as has been the case in many Muslim countries, will fail to yield the expected religious outcome of Islam as a *din*; a way of life. It will not only fail to project Weberian "substantive rationality" but will drift toward a "formal rationality," splitting the law from other parts of societal structure and rendering Islam a personal affair and an individual sociocultural project and not a complete way of life characteristic of pristine Islam. Second, Australia's Muslim population, although fast increasing, remains relatively small (340,392) compared to the total Australian population. This Muslim population, as I have discussed above, is also enormously heterogeneous, with members from around seventy different nations. They are divided not only along national, ethnic, and parochial lines, but also differ along sectarian and ideological lines. They operate independently and in isolation from each other. There is no general consensus on a variety of religious issues, and each Muslim group has its own distinct position on *Shari'a,* ranging from its status as a fixed legal system to its openness to reform to whether its implementation can be full or partial. This is further compounded by different interpretations of Islamic historicity, the sacred texts (Qur'ān and *hadith*), and classical literature on Islam. Also, disagreement exists relating to the design, formulation, and implementation of the *Shari'a*.

Within this total Muslim population, those who are calling for the formalization of the *Shari'a* are a very small group of Muslims, a vast majority of whom have to be relatively young because the first-generation Muslims (mature migrants) evidently were involved in community building and not in the process of formalizing *Shari'a* in Australia. Many Muslims in Australia are born here and almost half are 25 years of age or under.[40] By virtue of their young age, these Muslims who are calling for the formalization of *Shari'a* inevitably have only limited religious knowledge and experience, and their analytical skills are still developing. Of course, there exist some exceptions. Also, while a vast majority of these young Muslims espouse high moral virtues and ethical standards and take piety very seriously, they are still in the process of familiarizing themselves with and grasping the origins and evolution of *Shari'a*, jurisprudential knowledge, and the implementation of *Shari'a* in the manner undertaken during the period of pristine Islam. However, they are largely learning this not formally but as part of growing up in a Muslim family, and this is itself inherently problematic. They also require the training, skills, and experience needed (apparently no recognizable[41] Muslim institution exists that caters to these needs in Australia) to negotiate a complex process of formalizing the *Shari'a* with Australian power brokers, legal experts, and policymakers.

Third, many so-called *imams* (Muslim leaders) who support such an idea and are actively engaged in the process not only lack "Islamic knowledge and practice" but demonstrably don't cooperate and consult with each other and with the wider Muslim community. Not only this, but many qualified *imams* and *alims* (Muslim scholars) who are graduates of great Islamic centers of learning such as the University of Al-Azhar, trained in the classic Islamic jurisprudential methodologies. For example, the University of Al-Azhar, the great Sunni mosque-*madrasa*, although over a thousand years old and the most important center for higher learning, has been gradually modernized and reformed since the late nineteenth century.[42] Zubaida notes that

> [i]n 1961, under Nasir, the educational component was converted into a modern university, offering curricula in the religious sciences alongside modern faculties of science, arts and technology, and under its own rectorship. The shaykh of al-azhar, now appointed by the president, and not, as previously, chosen by his peers, presides over the religious institution. In effect, religious personnel were largely converted into state functionaries, and official religious authority firmly subordinated to the political directorate.[43]

According to Bernard Botiveau, during educational reform in 1961 the Faculty of Law at the University of Al-Azhar became the Faculty of *Shari'a* and Law.[44] The implication here is that the reform has significantly altered the historical role of Al-Azhar, whose central function and focus was to provide training in the expertise of the law, which is no longer the case. The effect of the reform has substantially weakened an important part of the religious authority of Al-Azhar. The reform process also has produced a sharp separation of the profession of the law and religious discipline and piety. The serious attempts by the modernizers to keep *'ibadat* (ritual) separate from *mu'amlat* (transactions) by suggesting two separate modes of application removes crucial facets of training and education of the jurists, that of religious conviction, ethical standards, moral virtue, and rectitude gained from regular and routine participation in a series of key religious rituals and practices within the confinement of a sacred institution. Consequently, individuals receiving training in this modern system inevitably seek to maintain its operation and existence because it is in their interests to do so or they have a vested interest in doing so. Even those lawyers and judges who are passionate revivalists and support a systematic Islamization of the law and the complete implementation of Islamic law often become disinclined to pursue the revival of the legal institutions of courts, *qāḍīs*, and juridical law (instead of state law typical of the early Islamic period), because of their fear of being taken over by the "progressive" and "modernist" lawyers and judges.

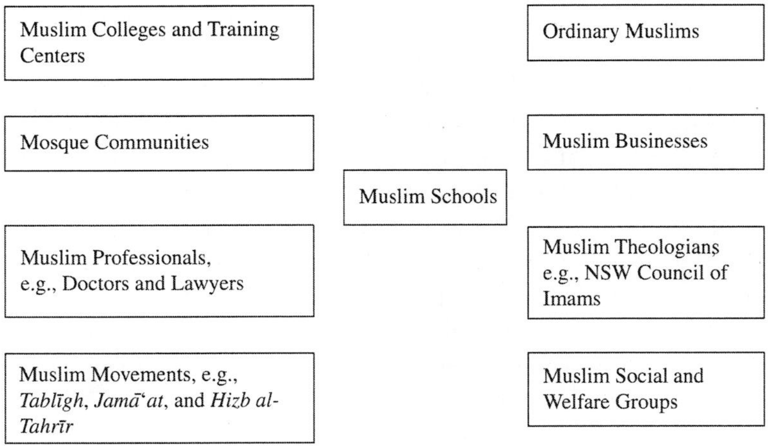

Figure 1: Muslim community organizations.

Fourth, Muslim organizations are not connected with each other at the operational level and, as Figure 1, no way exhaustive, shows, they operate independently.

Despite the fact that the above organizations provide a mixture of religious and nonreligious activities in the Muslim communities in Australia, there is no coordination of these activities between the organizations. In many instances these organizations are managed and run by Muslims with limited knowledge and practice of Islam. For example, Muslim schools in Australia teach the generic curriculum supplemented by Arabic and Islamic studies. Yet they are called Muslim or Islamic schools, giving the impression that they are religious schools providing a solid Islamic education as a pedagogical process. In fact, Muslim schools in Australia are secular institutions that operate with a corporate ethos.

These organizations represent Islam and are at the very forefront of Muslim activities. However, given the fact that there is not only an absence of coordination between the organizations and their activities, but an absence of any interaction between them, one can ask the question: how could the *Shari'a* be formalized in Australia? Which organizations will lead the charge for the formalization of *Shari'a,* and who will the *Shari'a* be for? Without consensus and cooperation among Muslims, particularly among bodies representing Islam and Muslims in Australia, any call for the formalization of the *Shari'a* will inevitably fail.

The call by (some) Muslims for a dual legal system through the formalization of *Shari'a* in Australia raises a critical issue of cultural and religious pluralism and is a test of freedom of religion in all the countries of the West in an era of postcolonial globalization. The West prides itself for being civilized, possessing enviable rationality, tolerance, compassion, and understanding. It purports to hold open values and to confer freedom of religion to all citizens. Under these provisions, Muslims who seek to pursue an "Islamic way of life" in full light of the *Shari'a* should be able to do so. However, in reality this is not the case. For example, when Muslims have sought to establish mosques, Muslim schools, or express their Muslimness through attire (*hijab* and *burqa*) and religious rituals (prayer at work), they have found that their citizenship rights have been challenged. When Muslim citizens have attempted to exercise their constitutional right to freedom of religion, they have often found that there is a limit to freedom of religion. The limit to freedom of religion sees them exercising only those Islamic practices and rituals that don't impact particularly upon public space; other practices and rituals are forced into the confinement of the domestic sphere.

Islam, however, is a way of life pervading both public and private spheres. When a limit is imposed on freedom of religion, Muslims seek, under the provisions of free society, the formalization of the *Shari'a* in order to fulfil their religious obligations and pursue Islam as a complete way of life. In a sense, then, the call by Muslims for a dual legal system through the formalization of *Shari'a* in Australia is a response to the limits on freedom of religion in Australia.

However, limiting of freedom of religion in Australia is not the sole problem of Muslims. As I outlined earlier, a vast majority of Muslims don't pursue lives based on *Shari'a*. They would first have to implement *Shari'a* at an individual level in terms of the fundamental principles of Islam through "higher *jihad*" and start a dialogue among themselves to iron out many ethnic, parochial, sectarian, and ideological differences that plague their social relationships in Australia as well as internationally. Muslims need to understand that the principal teaching of Islam is to surrender to the Will of Allah in totality and adhere to His commands on a consistent basis. Before *Shari'a* could be considered for formalization in Australia, Muslims will have to demonstrate a collective religiosity and true adherence to Islam both in private and public lives, and thus prove the utility and practical applicability of *Shari'a* for the betterment of society.

It is not disputed that a complete Islamic way of life requires a clear and firm legal foundation, but in the postmodern era in which life is enormously fragmentary and people are beholden to multiple identities, being a Muslim has many denotations; a monolithic Islam, as it once was, does not exist anywhere any more. Thus, like elsewhere, in Australia the sociological reality of Muslim living vividly reveals, to a large extent, a selective implementation of Islamic teaching and values and a close conformity to the Australian secular system through open participation in key institutions and social processes. If this is the Muslim reality, calling, by minority Muslims, for the dual legal system through the formalization of *Shari'a* in Australia is not only premature but sociologically unsustainable.

NOTES

1. Abdullah Ali, *Roman Transliteration of Holy Quran with Full Arabic Text* (Lahore: Sh. Muhammad Ashraf, 1938).

2. Ism'ail Raji al Faruqi, *The Cultural Atlas of Islam* (London: Al-Saadawi Publications, 1986), 246.

3. Wael Hallaq, *The Origins and Evolution of Islamic Law* (Cambridge: Cambridge University Press, 2005), 21.

4. Mohammad Kamali, *An Introduction to Shariah* (Kuala Lumpur: Ilhiah, 2006).

5. Malise Ruthven, *Islam in the World*, new ed. (London: Granta Books, 2006), 135.

6. Mawil Izzi Dien, *Islamic Law: From Historical Foundations to Contemporary Practice* (Edinburgh: Edinburgh University Press, 2004), 35.

7. Wael Hallaq, "From Regional to Personal Schools of Law? A Reevaluation," *Islamic Law and Society* 8, no. 1 (2001): 1–26.

8. Hallaq, *The Origins and Evolution of Islamic Law*.

9. Commonwealth of Australia, *1991 Census of Population and Housing*, Catalogue No. 2722.0, Australian Bureau of Statistics, Canberra, 1992; Commonwealth of Australia, *1996 Census of Population and Housing*, Catalogue No. 2901.0, Australian Bureau of Statistics, Canberra, 1997; Commonwealth of Australia, *2001 Census of Population and Housing*, Catalogue No. 2015.0, Australian Bureau of Statistics, Canberra, 2002; Commonwealth of Australia, *2006 Census of Population and Housing*, Catalogue No.2068.0, Australian Bureau of Statistics, Canberra, 2007.

10. Wafia Omar and Kirsty Allen, *The Muslims in Australia* (Canberra: Australian Government Publishing Service, 1997), 23.

11. Commonwealth of Australia, *2001 Census of Population and Housing*; Commonwealth of Australia, *2006 Census of Population and Housing*.

12. Abdullah Saeed, *Islam in Australia* (Crows Nest: George Allen and Unwin, 2003).

13. Ibid.

14. M. Jones, "The Years of Decline, Australian Muslims 1900–40," in *An Australian Pilgrimage: Muslims in Australia from the Seventeenth Century to the Present*, ed. M. Jones (Melbourne: Victoria Press,1993), 63–86.

15. Ibid.

16. Michael Humphrey, *Islam, Multiculturalism and Transnationalism: From the Lebanese Diaspora* (London: I. B. Tauris Publishers, 1998).

17. Gary Bouma, *Mosques and Muslim Settlement in Australia* (Canberra: Bureau of Immigration and Population Research, 1994).

18. Bilal Cleland, "The History of Muslims in Australia," in *Muslim Communities in Australia*, ed. A. Saeed and S. Akbarzadeh (Sydney: University of New South Wales Press, 2001), 12–32.

19. Humphrey, *Islam, Multiculturalism and Transnationalism*.

20. Amanda Wise and Jan Ali, *Muslim-Australians and Local Government: Grassroots Strategies to Improve Relations Between Muslim and Non-Muslim Australians*, Final Research Report, Department of Immigration and Citizenship and the Centre for Research on Social Inclusion (Sydney: Macquarie University, 2008).

21. Michael Humphrey, *Family, Work, and Unemployment: A Study of Lebanese Settlement in Sydney* (Canberra: Australian Government Publishing Service, 1984).

22. Humphrey, *Islam, Multiculturalism and Transnationalism*, 21.

23. Ibid.

24. Michael Humphrey, "Australian Islam, the New Global Terrorism and the Limits of Citizenship," in *Islam and the West: Reflections from Australia*, ed. S. Akbarzadeh and S. Yasmeen (Sydney: University of New South Wales Press, 2005), 132–148, 136.

25. Michael Humphrey, "Islam: A Test for Multiculturalism," *Asian Migrant* 2, no. 2 (1989): 48–56.

26. Ibid.

27. Gary Bouma, *Mosques and Muslim Settlement in Australia* (Canberra: Bureau of Immigration and Population Research, 1994).

28. Michael Humphrey, "Is This a Mosque Free-Zone? Islam and the State in Australia," *Migration Monitor* 12 (1989): 12–17.

29. Jones, "The Years of Decline, Australian Muslims 1900–40," 63–86.

30. Cleland, "The History of Muslims in Australia," 12–32.

31. Gary Bouma, Joan Daw, and Riffat Munawar, "Muslims Managing Religious Diversity," in *Muslim Communities in Australia*, ed. A. Saeed and S. Akbarzadeh (Sydney: University of New South Wales Press, 2001), 53–72, 69.

32. Ibid., 70.

33. Tariq Ramadan, "Islam and Muslims in Europe: A Silent Revolution Toward Rediscovery," in *Muslims in the West: From Sojourners to Citizens*, ed. Y. Haddad (Oxford: Oxford University Press, 2002), 158–166.

34. Ibid., 162.

35. Ibid., 159.

36. Ibid., 160.

37. Lars Pedersen, *Newer Islamic Movements in Western Europe* (London: Ashgate, 1999).

38. They are *Sunni*-based movements.

39. Jan Ali, "Islamic Revivalism: A Study of the Tablighi Jamaat in Sydney" (PhD diss., University of New South Wales, 2006).

40. Pamela Ryan, *Australia Deliberates: Muslims and Non-Muslims in Australia* (Canberra: Issues Deliberation Australia/America [IDA], 2007).

41. It is important to appreciate that although there are Muslim organizations or institutions of higher learning such as the Daar Aisha Shariah College in Lakemba in the south-west suburb of Sydney, they are not recognized by all Muslims or even by Australian authorities. Even the Australian Federation of Islamic Councils is not recognized by many Muslims although it is the national umbrella body.

42. Sami Zubaida, *Law and Power in the Islamic World* (London: I. B.Tauris, 2003).

43. Ibid., 159–60.

44. Bernard Botiveau, *Loi islamique et droit dans les societes arabes: Mutations des systemes juridiques du Moyen-Orient* (Paris and Aix-en-Provence: Karthala-IREMAM, 1993).

More Than One Law for All: Legal Pluralism in Southeast Asia[1]

Jamila Hussain

Faculty of Law, University of Technology, Australia

It is virtually an article of faith for politicians and lawmakers in common law countries that there must be "one law for all." For these people, equality under the law means that all people must be treated in exactly the same way by the legal system, regardless of differences in cultural background or religious belief. Among neighboring countries in Southeast Asia, this is not the case. Legal pluralism exists in Malaysia, with a formal system of *Shari'a* for Muslims and a separate system of *Shari'a* courts. Additionally, native courts exist to resolve problems relating to members of indigenous communities. In Indonesia, *Shari'a* courts exist alongside the civil courts to hear family law and inheritance matters relating to Muslims. In some areas of Indonesia, broader *Shari'a* laws and regulations have been introduced. Islamic finance flourishes in both countries with its own structures and regulations. *Adat* (customary) rules also continue to exist alongside the formal legal system. Thailand and the Philippines also have multiethnic and multireligious populations and at least some recognition of pluralism in their legal systems. Legal pluralism is not without its difficulties. There have been problems of jurisdiction, difficulties in deciding whether a person belongs in a particular category subject to a certain law, and questions of what to do when a person evinces a desire to leave a category and what to do with cases involving persons from two or more different legal categories. Despite these problems it can be argued that in Malaysia, at least, legal pluralism works reasonably well. This article examines the origin of legal pluralism in Malaysia, Indonesia, and Thailand and outlines ways in which governments have sought to deal with the challenges it presents.

It is virtually an article of faith for politicians and lawmakers in common law countries that there must be "one law for all." From this viewpoint, equality under the law means that all people must be treated in exactly the same way by the legal system, regardless of differences in cultural background, religious belief, or personal choice.

This idea, predominant in modern times, is a manifestation of legal universalism that imagines a homogenous citizenry who have uniform legal rights and obligations.[2] It does not take account of differences in personal beliefs, religious law, or of customary practices of different groups. Legal pluralism, on the other hand, regards ethnic and/or religious groups as one of the building blocks of a multicultural and multireligious society and recognizes their rights to be governed under the personal law of their communities, subject to the overriding state law in matters that are of common interest to the community as a whole.

Among neighboring countries in Southeast Asia, legal universalism is not the rule. Several varieties of legal pluralism exist, some formally recognized by the state, others informal. As one example, in Malaysia, there is a formal system of *Shari'a* (*Syariah*) for Muslims and a separate system of *Shari'a* courts.[3] Another tier of native courts exists to resolve problems relating to members of indigenous communities. As a second example, in Indonesia, there is no formal parallel system of *Shari'a* courts alongside the civil courts, but family law and inheritance matters relating to Muslims are heard in religious courts that are part of the state system but apply Islamic law. In some areas of Indonesia, broader *Shari'a* laws and regulations have been introduced. Islamic finance flourishes in both countries with its own structures and regulations alongside ordinary secular commercial laws. *Adat* (customary) rules also continue to exist alongside the formal legal system.

In Thailand the Muslim minority has gained informal recognition of their obligation to follow the *Shari'a* in matters of personal law, but this is not as extensively or formally recognized as in Malaysia or Indonesia. Singapore, Brunei, and the Philippines each have a separate system of *Shari'a* courts and recognition of Islamic personal law applying to Muslims.

Legal pluralism is not without its difficulties. There have been problems of jurisdiction, difficulties in deciding whether a person belongs in a particular category subject to a certain law, and questions of what to do when a person evinces a desire to leave a category and what to do with cases involving persons from two or more different legal categories. Despite these problems it can be argued that given the circumstances, legal pluralism works reasonably well and is in fact the only practical solution in multiethnic, multireligious countries like those in Southeast Asia.

This article examines the origin of legal pluralism in Southeast Asia, and using the examples of Malaysia, Indonesia, and Thailand, outlines ways in which their governments have sought to deal with the challenges it presents.

LEGAL PLURALISM: A HISTORICAL PERSPECTIVE

Brian Tamanaha has pointed out that legal pluralism was common in Europe before the rise of the modern nation-state, which appropriated law as its own monopoly.[4] In the Medieval period, a great variety of laws—customary law, feudal law, church law, merchant law (*lex mercatoria*), and revived Roman law—all existed in the same space, each with its own courts competing with others. An assortment of different people served as judges, applying different laws to different litigants in accordance with their ethnicity and cultural traditions. In Spain (Muslim Al Andalus), Jewish and Islamic laws were also practiced and coexisted with laws applicable to Christian inhabitants.[5]

This situation existed for hundreds of years, until the multiple kingdoms, duchies, and other fragmentary entities in Europe were finally brought under the control of the modern nation-state as we know it, and state bureaucracies were established to administer a formal centralized law. Today, however, some argue that the principle of "one law for all" is not equitable and that with the growing multicultural character of European societies, there should be some flexibility in allowing cultural minorities to observe their own personal laws.[6]

Legal pluralism was by no means confined to medieval Europe. In the Middle East, India, and other territories that came to form parts of Islamic empires that rose and flourished between the eighth and eighteenth centuries CE, legal pluralism was the norm. Here, Islamic law was applicable to all the Muslim subjects. However, following the *Shari'a* rule that the forced conversion of people who follow another recognized prophet is not allowed,[7] those non-Muslim people living peacefully within the empire were regarded as "protected minorities" (*dhimmis*). In consideration of payment of a tax known as *jizya*, they were exempted from service in the armed forces and granted the protection of the state. They were allowed to keep their own languages and customs, to open and maintain their own educational institutions, and to practice their faith freely, provided they did not cause offense to Muslims.

Non- Muslims were allowed to be governed by their own religious law; they made and administered their own personal laws and enforced them through their own courts. At the same time they were exempted from Islamic laws that prohibited Muslims from making wine and eating and trading in pork.[8] The institution of this *dhimmi* system has been much criticized, since it was not always administered fairly, but it did allow minorities, mostly Christians, Jews, and Zoroastrians, to live subject to their own religious laws. In India, under the Mughal emperor Akbar, Hindus, who unlike Jews and Christians did not fall into the category of "people of the book," were allowed to regulate their own communities with their own law and institutions.[9]

The Ottoman empire, which endured from 1299 to 1923, included many different ethnic and religious groups—Arabs, both Sunni and Shia, Arab

Christians in their many varieties, Jews, non-Arab Christians in Greece and the Balkans, Armenians, and many others. Under the Ottoman *millet* system, in accordance with Islamic principles on the treatment of non-Muslim minorities, each of these groups was able to organize its own internal affairs. The *millets* had considerable powers. They were headed by their own religious leaders, could make their own laws, collect taxes, and maintain their own courts to hear disputes between members of their communities and deal with criminal matters within the community. Disputes involving Muslims were referred to the Ottoman courts. Defense, foreign policy, and other matters of universal importance to the state, of course, remained under the control of the Ottoman sultan.

Instituted by Sultan Mehmet II after his conquest of Constantinople in 1453, the *millet* system endured until at least the late nineteenth century. Then the declining Ottoman empire was forced to allow various European powers to assume the "protection" of various allied ethnicities within it. Ideas of nationalism promoted the idea of each ethnic group having its own state. By most accounts the *millet* system had numerous advantages and worked well for many centuries.[10] Its legacy has been retained in the modern Middle East, whereas in most countries, there are separate secular and religious courts. The religious courts deal with family law and inheritance, and separate courts exist for each of the different major religious communities. This is the case in Egypt, Lebanon, Jordan, and Israel. Although the system has disadvantages, it shows that this kind of legal pluralism is capable of enduring in a way that is at least reasonably satisfactory to most of the people governed by it.

In contrast to the recent legal universalizing tendencies in Europe, colonial governments resulted in an increase in legal pluralism in colonies acquired by European powers in Asia and elsewhere. This often overlaid existing legal pluralisms, which had developed from different waves of migration, religious conversion, and the persistence of long established cultural rules. In most cases, colonial powers were interested in their colonies principally for the pursuit of trade and profit. They imposed, directly or indirectly, as much of their own legal systems as they considered necessary to meet their commercial objectives, but mostly left the personal laws of the local population alone, since there was no advantage for them in forcing changes in laws concerning marriage, divorce, and succession relating to the native population.

In some cases, indigenous judges continued to apply existing law to local populations, particularly in these fields. In other places and times, British or European judges struggled with and sometimes failed to understand the intricacies of Hindu, Muslim, Chinese, and other local laws, which differed not only from country to country but also from region to region and between ethnic and religious groups within those countries. Tamanaha points out, "in many locations, what resulted was a dual legal system with various complex mixtures and combinations, and mutual influences."[11]

ORIGINS OF LEGAL PLURALISM IN SOUTHEAST ASIA

In Southeast Asia, colonial laws were overlaid upon existing local legal systems, themselves a mix of long-established customary law and more recent influences from periods of Hindu or Buddhist dominance. These periods were followed in Malaysia and Indonesia by the widespread acceptance of Islam, which brought its own law but did not succeed in eradicating entirely either the customary *(adat)* or some later Hindu and Buddhist practices in areas where they were established. New migrations added further religious and ethnic influences to this mix.

Even before the coming of the Europeans, Southeast Asia, situated on the trade routes between China, India, and Europe, was a prosperous center attracting traders from the Middle East, India, China, and the rest of the Asian region. Some of these traders settled, bringing with them their families, religions, cultures, and laws. The situation was further complicated by the migration of many Chinese during the nineteenth and early twentieth centuries, who were displaced by civil or political strife at home or seeking work and business opportunities in a more congenial environment. Between 1860 and 1931 the Chinese population of Indonesia, Malaya, Thailand, and Singapore increased from about 700,000 to 3.8 million, a rate of increase far greater than that of the indigenous population.[12] As these migrants came from a number of different provinces in China, they brought with them several varieties of Chinese customary law.

During the British period in Malaya, the British brought Tamils from India, mostly as indentured laborers, to work in the tin mines and on the rubber plantations. Some migrants also came from the north of India in search of business ventures. In this way, a variety of Indian laws and customs were introduced to an already complex mix.

Malaysia

"[C]ontemporary Malaysian law . . . is a hybrid law, drawing its ideas from many sources."[13] This is a result of Malaysia's colorful and varied history. As early as the fourth century CE, Indian traders and settlers introduced Hindu and Buddhist influences, which mingled with and became ingrained in the existing *adat*, or customary law, of the indigenous inhabitants. *Adat* was mostly unwritten and varied from place to place, being passed down the generations in the form of oral verses and sayings.

In about the fourteenth century CE, the coming of Islam brought the *Shari'a* and the *fiqh* of the Shafii school, which largely managed to reach an accommodation with local *adat,* adding a new layer of pluralism. Some *adat* conflicted with the rules of Islamic law and were discarded. Other *adat* could be accepted, or modified to become acceptable, on the principle that custom may be recognized in Islamic law if it does not contradict the Quran or the Sunnah. The spread of Islamic law was uneven. Some of the classical *Shari'a* texts were known and in use, but did not by any means constitute a universal legal system. The *Undang-Undang Melaka* and the *Undang-Undang Laut Melaka* were two legal digests that were in force toward the end of the period of the powerful Malacca sultanate. They reflected both the local *adat* and Islamic law of the Shafii school.[14] The first digest dealt with matters such as the responsibilities of the ruler, civil and criminal penalties, and family law. The latter dealt with maritime regulations. In East Malaysia—now Sarawak and Sabah—the customary laws of native tribes prevailed, with an overlay of Islamic law where Islam had been adopted.

Thus when the British arrived, legal pluralism was already well established in Malaysia. In 1786 the British gained control of Penang through an agreement with the sultan of Kedah. In 1807, English law was introduced there through the Charter of Justice and became the law of the land. English law was similarly introduced in the other Straits Settlements, Malacca and Singapore, and as the various Malay states were gradually brought under British "protection," English law spread there too, displacing and downgrading Malay-Muslim laws that had previously been in force. The jurisdiction of the *Shari'a* courts was limited to marriage, divorce, and other personal matters, and when the British style hierarchical courts were set up, the *Shari'a* courts were placed at the bottom of the hierarchy with little in the way of funding and resources.

Like their colonial confederates in Indonesia—the Dutch—the British were primarily interested in trade and exploiting the resources to increase the economic power of the homeland. Their intervention in local affairs was mainly to safeguard their business interests.[15] They were prepared to leave alone most of the customs and laws of the local inhabitants so long as these did not have a detrimental effect on trade, so customary and religious laws continued in areas such as family law and inheritance.

Some customary laws have survived up to the present, although often in changed format, reduced to text and published as modern Western legislation. Much of this transition occurred during the British colonial period.[16] Even today there is no common customary law in Malaysia, although the need to recognize cultural diversity conflicts with the need for uniformity in civil and criminal law. Some aspects of customary and religious law have been modified and others have disappeared. The influence of customary law generally seems to be waning, while that of Islamic law is expanding.[17] Today, Islamic personal law applies to Muslims regardless of ethnicity and native law to those classified as natives in Sabah and Sarawak.

In the field of public law, "English law came into Malaysia as a tide, at first a gentle movement in a few places and then as a powerful surge challenging the entire coast and its estuaries."[18] English law was to be applied, but only insofar as the religions, manners, and customs of the inhabitants would permit. Appropriate customary laws could be accommodated, including polygamous marriages according to Islamic law and what the British believed was Chinese and Hindu custom. Strictly speaking, the Charters of Justice promulgated by the British applied only in Penang, Malacca, and Singapore, but the principles were extended to all Malay states as they came under British control.[19] For non-Muslims, personal religious laws in the area of family law have now been replaced by the *Law Reform (Marriage and Divorce) Act* 1976, legislation that is based on a British model. This act abolished polygamous marriages for non-Muslims but did not affect the rights of Muslim men to marry more than one wife, as permitted under Islamic law and reflected in the Islamic Family Law enactments of the various states and territories.

There are still a few minor areas where customary law related to family law is recognized. It also remains applicable to some aspects of land ownership.[20] The new legislation has reduced legal pluralism to the extent that all non-Muslims are now treated alike in family law matters, and cultural diversity has thus necessarily been lessened.

Malays in peninsular Malaysia are governed by *adat* as well as Islamic law and the general law. The *adat* varies, is largely unwritten except in Sarawak, and the techniques and rules of evidence of the civil courts are often used to make determinations of *adat* contained in proverbs and common sayings. *Adat perpateh* is a distinct matrilineal tradition relating to land. It is practiced in Negeri Sembilan and parts of Malacca and has been given statutory recognition.

In Sabah and Sarawak, Malay customary law can be applied to Malays and native customary law applied to non-Malay natives, such as the Dayak and Iban and similar tribes. In Sarawak, Chinese customary law is still recognized in legislation such as the *Chinese Marriage Ordinance*. There is a statutory definition of "natives" in the Federal Constitution Art 161A, clause 7, which applies in Sarawak. In Sabah, section 3 of *Interpretation (Definition of Native)* Ordinance of 1952 applies, amended in 1958. A person claiming to be a native may apply to the Native Court for an official declaration that they are indeed a native. Native customary rights over land are gradually being eroded in Sarawak by pressure for development.[21]

In Sarawak and Sabah, Native Courts are state courts separate from the federal system. In Sarawak they have jurisdiction in matters relating to native law and custom. There is a hierarchy of six courts, the lowest being the Headman's court and the highest the Native Court of Appeal. In Sabah there is a similar system with three tiers. Where a matter is sexual or matrimonial and parties are from different communities, the law of the woman's community applies.[22]

Muslim Malaysians, who constitute about 60 percent of the population, are governed in matters of personal law by Islamic law, with no opportunity to opt out. The Federal Constitution[23] defines who is Malay and includes being Muslim as an essential attribute. Islamic law also applies to non-Malay Muslims. A parallel hierarchy of Islamic courts (*Shari'a* or *Syariah* courts) exists alongside the civil system. *Shari'a* courts are presided over by a *kadi*, a judge trained in Islamic law, and there is a *Shari'a* Court of Appeal.

According to the Federal Constitution, Islam is the religion of the Federation[24] and enjoys a special status, although Buddhism, Hinduism, and Christianity are also practiced and religious conflict is fairly rare. The introduction of Islamic finance and the establishment of Bank Islam in 1983 introduced a new element of pluralism into the financial system, since disputes relating to *Shari'a* contracts and other aspects of Islamic finance must be decided according to Islamic law. Malaysia is now one of the world's leading hubs of Islamic finance.

However, the extent to which Islamic jurisprudence should be incorporated into the general legal system remains a sensitive issue.[25] In recent times there has been increased pressure from sections of the Muslim population for aspects of Islamic law to be included as part of the general legal system and thus applied to all citizens. This has created tensions between Muslims and non-Muslim communities. Some writers have attributed this tension, at least in part, to the increasing influence of Wahhabi-inspired literal interpretations of Islam imported from the Middle East since the 1980s.[26] This has led to a decline in the importance of *adat* in Malay community life and so has lessened pluralism.

Indonesia

Indonesia is not an Islamic state, but is a predominantly Muslim country[27] where, despite the predominance of Islam, six different religions are currently recognized.[28] The overriding principle is *Pancasila*, which requires belief in God but does not specify which god a person must believe in. Efforts to include a requirement that Muslim Indonesians must be subject to *Shari'a* were defeated in the days following independence and have not gained acceptance since. Numerous Islamist parties have emerged in Indonesia since the end of Soeharto's dictatorship, but none have been particularly successful in the polls. Nevertheless, Islam is deeply embedded in the life of the population.

Indonesia is also a country of many and varied ethnicities among its population of 230 million. There are said to be 19 different types of *adat* and a wide variety of local languages and customs. Both *adat* and Islamic law were well established before the advent of Dutch colonialism, although the latter was strong in some areas such as Aceh and barely noted in others such as the eastern islands, which became predominantly Christian.

In the course of time, the Dutch established their own variety of legal pluralism. Dutch people and other Europeans, and people such as the Japanese deemed to be honorary Europeans, were governed by Dutch law. There was another law for "foreign orientals," mostly the Chinese and Arabs, and the bulk of the "native" population was governed by a "native" law. Islamic law was regarded as a threat to Dutch supremacy and was deliberately marginalized—a policy which continued under the dictators Soekarno and Soeharto.[29] Islamic law came to be restricted to family law and inheritance. Criminal law was meant to be uniform and applied to everyone. According to some writers, the division among population groups is still reflected in the private law system.[30]

Indonesian law today is based on the civil law system, but it is a curious mixture of old Dutch statutes (some written in Dutch and thus incomprehensible to the bulk of the population), *adat*, Islamic law, Presidential decrees, and modern statutes, some of which conflict with other sections of the law. Overlapping jurisdictions result in disputes between civil and religious courts over which has the right to decide a case. Efforts to unify the system have, as yet, not been successful, and some such efforts have turned out to be counterproductive in practice.

The law relating to land is an example. Much land, especially in rural areas, is still subject to *adat* rights that are not easily converted into Western-style land titles, since there has been no system of registration or of easily establishing individual ownership. There are conflicting provisions in some legislation and ambiguities in government policies. The Agrarian law of 1960 provided a dualism in that ownership of land might depend on the category of the owner, but his use of the land might depend on the category of the land, whether forestry or mining or other type.[31] According to some authors, the attempt to legislate a uniform national agrarian law has left some Indonesians with unrecognized or tenuous interests in land and vulnerable to eviction without compensation.[32] This has impacted primarily on the poor and rural communities.

In family law, there have been tensions between the Marriage Law and the uncodified Islamic law that traditionally governed marriage and divorce for Muslims. In the past, there were separate laws for Christians and for Chinese and Europeans. In 1974, an attempt was made to modernize the law on marriage by promulgating one law for all Indonesians regardless of religion and ethnicity. It was proposed to restrict polygamy and improve women's rights, allow mixed marriages, and lessen the jurisdiction of the religious courts. The initial bill was amended in response to protests by conservative Muslims, who opposed provisions that contravened Islamic law provisions as set out in the Quran. A compromise was reached and the current marriage Law, no. 1 of 1974, passed. In spite of intensive efforts by the government to enforce the statutory requirements of the act, there is some evidence that for many Indonesians social and religious recognition of their marriage is still more important than obtaining legal recognition from the state, and some continue to marry without complying with the statute.[33] Such marriages are recognized as valid by society and religious leaders despite failure to comply with official law.

The government, however, also wished to be seen as upholding Islamic law. In 1985, it commissioned a group of prominent Islamic scholars to make a compilation of the Islamic law relating to marriage, divorce, and inheritance (*Kompilasi Hukum Islam*) as an official reference to be used by the courts in determining family law matters. This was promulgated by President Soeharto as Presidential Decree No. 1 of 1991.The Compilation, in codified form, gives expression to the *fiqh* of the Shafii school, which is followed in Indonesia. It also includes as sources some texts of other madhabs, existing *yurisprudensi* and *fatawa* of the *ulama* (religious scholars),[34] as well as provisions such as minimum age of marriage that are not specified in the uncodified *Shari'a*. As Cammack and his coauthors point out, the struggle for control of family law practices in Indonesia demonstrates the inability of the state to alter long-established marriage practices in the face of deeply held religious convictions.[35]

Indonesia, unlike Malaysia, does not have a formal parallel system of religious courts. The religious courts are part of the state system and have jurisdiction over family law, deciding disputes largely in accordance with Islamic law. In 2006, Article 49, Law No. 3 broadened the jurisdiction of the Religious court to include *Shari'a* banking and economy. Both Muslims and non-Muslims can have recourse to the court in both family law and financial matters.

In some areas of Indonesia, different types of law appear to coexist without significant conflict. Erman Rajagukguk points out that on the small island of Lombok—where the majority of the three million inhabitants are Muslim—some villages follow *adat* in inheritance cases, even where it conflicts with Islamic law or state law. Others adhere to Islamic law, and other individuals choose to approach the state district court for a determination of their issues.[36] This can result in radically different outcomes, especially for women, when *adat* does not recognize female inheritance rights and Islamic law does not always give women equal rights with men.

Regional autonomy laws introduced in 1999 (revised in 2004) have complicated the issue. These laws gave local governments the right to promulgate laws for their own areas. In places where this opportunity was taken up, the practice led to a greater variety of pluralism. Some 22 local authorities used the opportunity to include strict *Shari'a* rules in their by-laws in relation to dress and public behavior.[37] In addition, the settlement of the long-running separatist insurgency in Aceh in 2001 included the right for Aceh to adopt *Shari'a* as its law. A provincial *Shari'a* court was added to the local *Shari'a* courts already in existence. *Shari'a qanun* (law codes) were introduced, regulating dress and observance of religious obligations, enforced by *Shari'a* police. Controversially, in 2009 the regional parliament passed a law to implement

Shari'a criminal law, including punishments such as stoning for adultery, but the incoming governor refused to sign it into law.[38]

Thailand

The majority population in Thailand is Thai-speaking Buddhist. However, in the four southern provinces the majority consists of Malay- (*Yawi-*) speaking Muslims who have more in common with their Malay coreligionists across the border than with Thai fellow citizens.[39] This political division came about when, in 1909, the British concluded the Anglo-Thai treaty with Siam[40] recognizing the four Malay- (*Yawi-*) speaking Muslim provinces as part of Siam (modern Thailand).

Relations between the two communities have not always been cordial. At various times, the policies of the Thai government have tended to marginalize the Muslim population. After the 1909 treaty, special legislation allowed Muslims in defined geographical areas to conduct their family law in accordance with *Shari'a*. Islamic family courts were established by Thai authorities, with judges chosen from respected local religious figures. Islamic law was practiced alongside Thai national law.[41] However, moves by successive Thai governments to impose Thai cultural uniformity occurred from time to time and were seen by the Muslims of the southern provinces as a form of internal colonization.[42] Attempts were made to impose the Thai language and to close religious schools. Muslims were required to adopt Thai names and cease using Muslim names. Uprisings occurred. The four southern provinces remained poor, with little economic or cultural development. Police and government officials sent to the south did not speak *Yawi* and could not communicate with local people. After World War II, there was a period of intense Thai nationalism when it was government policy to settle and integrate Buddhists in the southern provinces and suppress local Muslim separatists.

However, during the period when Thaksin Shiniwatra was Prime Minister, matters went from bad to worse. In 2004, there was an escalation of violence that broke down the relationship between Muslim and Buddhist communities. Buddhist *wats* were militarized, military monks appeared,[43] and there was an oppressive use of force by the Thai army. Martial law was imposed, and 3,500 people lost their lives in the fighting.[44]

After the 2006 coup, in which Thaksin lost power, the new government distanced itself from Thaksin's policies. In November 2006 the new Prime Minister, Surayad Chulanont, made a formal commitment to recognize *Shari'a* law. This was followed in June 2009 by an announcement by Prime Minister Abhisit Vejjajiva that Thailand was considering allowing more local autonomy and extending *Shari'a* law.[45]

The southern provinces of Thailand remain a work in progress. *Shari'a* rules are permitted for the settlement of family and inheritance disputes in the four southern provinces, but Muslims living elsewhere in Thailand must conform to state law. Requests from Muslims to extend the use of *Shari'a* to all Muslims have so far not borne fruit.

Legal pluralism exists in Thailand in a limited and troubled form, apparently accepted by the state only as a way of curbing the forces of separatism and insurgency.

SOME ISSUES IN LEGAL PLURALISM IN SOUTHEAST ASIA

Legal pluralism has advantages in that it allows discrete communities to regulate their societies in accordance with their own religious or cultural laws. There are, however, disadvantages.

Inevitably, legal pluralism results in some conflict between different legal systems. A classic case in Malaysia was that of *Maria Hertogh.*[46] This case arose shortly after the end of World War II. The then Dutch East Indies (modern Indonesia) had been occupied by the Japanese. Maria Hertogh, a child of Dutch parents, had been entrusted to the care of a Malay lady during the war and had been brought up as a Muslim in Terengganu. After the war her parents sought her out and attempted to reclaim her. By the time the matter reached the Court of Appeal she had been married to a Malay husband. It was argued that as a Muslim, under Islamic law, she was *sui juris* and her marriage was legitimate, even though she was under the minimum age of marriage in the country of her parents' domicile, Holland. The court applied English conflict of laws principles to what was essentially an interpersonal conflict, declared her marriage invalid, her domicile to be that of her father, and returned her to her parents in Holland. This caused enormous offense to the Malay Muslim population and riots followed. As Wu points ou, "One must never underestimate the negative impact of applying imported laws to local situations."[47]

There have been numerous other cases involving conversions or putative conversions. Another Malay case of note was *Teoh Eng Huat v. Kadhi Pasir Mas and Anor.*[48] In this case, a seventeen-year-old girl from a Buddhist family purported to convert to Islam. Her father applied to the court seeking a declaration that as her father and lawful guardian he had the right to determine her religion. The Supreme court agreed that the father had this right, although by the time the matter was decided, the girl had turned eighteen and was able to decide her religion for herself. Other cases have involved conversion of children by one parent and the right to bury deceased persons according to a particular religion.[49]

There are also conflicts between legal systems within the same jurisdiction. A "battle of jurisdiction" was waged for many years in Malaysia to determine the authority of the *Shari'a* system against that of the common law courts. In

1988, the Malaysian constitution was amended to include a new clause (1A) to Article 121. This provided that, henceforth, the High Court would have no jurisdiction over matters that fell within the jurisdiction of the *Shari'a* courts. As Wu points out, this resolves the problem where both parties to an action are Muslims, but the situation is not so clear cut where one party is a non-Muslim and therefore not under the jurisdiction of the *Shari'a* court. In any event, *Shari'a* courts must have been invested with jurisdiction in accordance with the State List in the federal constitution.[50]

The dilemma for the courts in trying to reconcile two systems is well illustrated by the recent Singapore case of *Shafeeg bin Salim Talib and anor v. Fatimah bte Abud bin Talib and ors*.[51] As in Malaysia, Singapore has a parallel system of *Shari'a* law for its Muslim population. In this case the court had to decide whether the right of survivorship in the civil law took precedence over the Islamic law of inheritance. The deceased, a Singapore Muslim of Yemeni descent, died intestate. The deceased had owned a flat in joint tenancy with his wife. She transferred the flat to herself and her two children who had converted to Christianity, and therefore they no longer qualified as persons entitled to inherit under Islamic law. Islamic law does not recognize a right of survivorship. The court held that Section 112 of the *Administration of Muslim Law Act*, which stated that the estate of a deceased Muslim should be distributed according to Muslim law, was concerned with the distribution of the assets of a deceased Muslim, not with the determination of the assets that constitute the estate. The determination was to be made under civil law, not Muslim law, and therefore the half share automatically fell under the ownership of the surviving joint tenant and did not form part of the estate of the deceased.

Many cases in Malaysia have involved attempts by Muslims to renounce Islam. These persons have claimed that as they were no longer Muslims, they could not be dealt with by the *Shari'a* court.[52] The court rejected this argument where the parties had committed an offense before purporting to renounce Islam. In the Lina Joy case,[53] it was held that a Muslim wishing to renounce Islam must obtain permission from a *Shari'a* court to leave Islam. Apostasy is a criminal offense in some states, and *Shari'a* courts have the power to send a person to a rehabilitation center for a period of up to one year. This decision casts doubt on the constitutional guarantee of religious freedom under Article 11.

Questions have arisen in other cases as to whether a person falls within the category claimed. A question of whether a person qualifies as a native was considered in the case of *Liew Siew Yin v. District Officer Jesselton* in 1959. It appeared that religion is not a required criterion in the definition, but a person must be recognized as a member of a native community or as a member of a tribe named in the definition. On the other hand, where a deceased person was claimed to be a Muslim and therefore subject to Islamic law, the court held that it was not necessary to establish that he practiced the rituals of the faith.[54]

A criticism leveled at legal pluralism by Western observers is that these systems do not result in equal treatment for litigants. Pertinent examples are that of inheritance cases in Lombok mentioned above. A woman may receive nothing—apart from some jewelry and household goods—if the estate is distributed according to *adat*. She may receive half as much as her brother if it is distributed according to Islamic law and an equal share if she goes to the civil courts. In other cases, *adat* or Islamic law may preserve rights that are not recognized by the civil law, for example, a woman's right to *mahr* (*mas kahwin* in Southeast Asia), the marriage gift that a Muslim husband must give his bride.

In the ethnically and religiously diverse societies of Southeast Asia it would be difficult, if not impossible, to find one uniform set of laws that would be acceptable and just to all. Unlike the largely secular populations in Western countries, Southeast Asian societies are still profoundly religious, and it is of paramount importance to many people that they conform to religious and/or cultural laws. In these circumstances, some degree of legal pluralism is really the only practical option.

NOTES

1. Geographically, Australia lies on the southern border of Asia. Its closest northern neighbors are the states of Southeast Asia—Indonesia, Malaysia, Singapore, the Philippines, and Thailand, as well as the new nations of East Timor and Papua New Guinea.

2. Susanne Hoeher Rudolph and Lloyd I. Rudolph, "Living with Difference in India," in *Religion and Personal Law in India*, ed. Gerald James Larson, 2001, http://politicalscience.uchicago.edu/faculty/rudolphs/living-with-difference.pdf

3. "*Shari'a*" is an Arabic word, which is transliterated in a number of different ways in Roman letters. In Southeast Asia, it is normally spelled "Syariah."

4. Brian Z Tamanaha, "Understanding Legal Pluralism: Past to Present, Local to Global," *Sydney Law Review* 30 (2008): 375.

5. Ibid., 378.

6. Pearl and Menski argue that failure to do so results in the development of informal hybrid legal systems widely observed by ethnic minorities outside the formal legal system. They have identified the concept of "Angrezi Shariat" as the hybrid system of personal laws practiced by many Muslims in Britain. David Pearl and Werner Menski, *Muslim Family Law* (London: Sweet & Maxwell, 1998).

7. W. Montgomery Watt, *Islamic Political Thought* (Edinburgh: Edinburgh University Press, 1969), 50.

8. 'Abdur Rahman I Doi, *Non-Muslims under Shari'ah* (Kuala Lumpur: A. S. Nordeen, 1990), 51.

9. BBC, *Religions–Mughal Empire*, 2009, http://www.bbc.co.uk/religion/religions/islam/history/mughalempire_1.shtml

10. Watt, *Islamic Political Thought*, 51.

11. Tamanaha, "Understanding Legal Pluralism," 384.

12. Jamie Mackie, "Introduction" in *Sojourners and Settlers Histories of Southeast Asia and the Chinese*, ed. Anthony Reid (Honolulu: University of Hawaii Press, 1996), xii.

13. Min Aun Wu, *The Malaysian Legal System* (Kuala Lumpur: Pearson, 2005), 212.

14. Ahmad Ibrahim and Ahilemah Joned, *The Malaysian Legal System* (Kuala Lumpur: Dewan Behasa dan Pustaka, 1987), 17.

15. Abdul Monir Yaacob, "*Shari'a* Courts in Malaysia: Past, Present and Future" *The Administration of Islamic Laws*, ed. Ahmad Mohamed Ibrahim and Abdul Monir Yaacob (Kuala Lumpur: IKIM, 1997), 24.

16. Wu, *The Malaysian Legal System*, 214.

17. Ibid., 213.

18. R. H. Hickling, *Malaysian Law* (Kuala Lumpur: Professional [Law] Books Publishers, 1987), 114.

19. Wu, *The Malaysian Legal System*, 214.

20. Ibid., 216.

21. Ibid., 240.

22. S 6 (3) Sabah Native Courts Enactment 1992.

23. Malaysian Federal Constitution, art. 160.

24. Malaysian Federal Constitution, art. 3, sec. 1.

25. Wu, *The Malaysian Legal System*, 210.

26. Lily Zubaidah Rahim, *Representing and Misrepresenting Islam: The Discursive Struggle Between Literal and Liberal Islam in Southeast Asia* (Melbourne: Nautilus Institute RMIT, 2006), 12.

27. Approximately 85% of Indonesians are estimated to be Muslims.

28. Islam, Buddhism, Hinduism, Catholicism, Protestant Christianity, and Confucianism.

29. Tim Lindsey and Mas Achmad Santosa, "The Trajectory of Law Reform in Indonesia," in *Indonesia, Law and Society,* ed. Tim Lindsey (Sydney: Federation Press, 2008), 8.

30. Ms. Herliana, "Legal Pluralism in Indonesia: An Advantage or Disadvantage to the Society?" (paper presentation, ASLI conference, Kuala Lumpur, 2010).

31. Ibid.

32. Daniel Fitzpatrick,"Beyond Dualism: Land Acquisition and Law in Indonesia," in *Indonesia, Law and Society* (2008), 224–26.

33. Mark Cammack, Lawrence A. Young, and Tim Heaton, "Legislating Social Change in an Islamic Society: Indonesia's Marriage Law," in *Indonesia, Law and Society* (2008), 302–03.

34. M. B. Hooker, "The State and Syariah in Indonesia 1945–1995" in *Indonesia, Law and Society* (Sydney: Federation Press, 1999), 106.

35. Cammack, Young, and Heaton, "Legislating Social Change," 308.

36. Erman Rajagukguk, "Legal Pluralism in the Multicultural Society of Lombok Island," (paper presentation, ASLI conference, Kuala Lumpur, 2010).

37. Geoff Thompson, "Conflict over *Shari'a* Law in Aceh," September 1, 2006, http://www.abc.net.au/pm/content/2006/s1731262.htm

38. Mark Colvin, "Future of *Shari'a* Uncertain in Aceh," June 14, 2010, http://www.abc.net.au/pm/content/2010/s2926616.htm?site=not-regionalised&source=rss

39. In the four southern provinces the Muslim population is at least 50% of the total population.

40. The former name of Thailand.

41. Peter Leyland, "Thailand's Troubled South: Examining the Case for Devolution from a Comparative Perspective," *Asian Law* 11 (2009), 4.

42. Michel Gilquin, *The Muslims of Thailand*, trans. Michael Smithies (Chiang Mai, Thailand: Silkworm Books, 2002).

43. Leyland, "Thailand's Troubled South," 9.

44. Ibid.

45. Haslinda Amin and Daniel Ten Kate, "Thailand May Extend *Shari'a* Law in Violence Ridden Muslim South," June 22, 2009, http://www.bloomberg.com/apps/news?pid=newsarchive&sid=ay7noiDdsTm0

46. MLJ 215 (1950); see also Ahmad Ibrahim, "From Nadra to Susie Teoh," *IIUM Law Journal* 1, http://lib.iiu.edu.my/mom2/cm/content/view/view.jsp?key=pIrQfamSOvVIKamxCSwpVFg8qlEsAIKT20080115152517484

47. Wu, *The Malaysian Legal System*, 218.

48. 2 MLJ 300 (1990).

49. Soon Singh v. Perbuhan Kebajikan Malaysia (Perkim) Kedah, 2 C.L.J 107 (1994).

50. Wu, *The Malaysian Legal System*, 202.

51. SGCA 11(2010).

52. *Kamariah bte Ali dan lain-lain v. Kerajaan Negeri Kelantan, Malaysia dan satu lagi* 3 MLJ 657 (2002); quoted in Wu, *The Malaysian Legal System*, 204.

53. *Lina Joy v. Majlis Agama Islam Wilayah Persekutuan* (30.5.2007).

54. *Re Mohamed Said Nabi deceased* 1 MLJ 121 (1936).

The Social Construction of Legal Pluralism

James T. Richardson

Grant Sawyer Center for Justice Studies, University of Nevada, Reno, Nevada

This article focuses on historical conditions and sociological variables that contribute to or impede the development of religious freedom. One major set of variables focuses on characteristics of legal and judicial systems. Another set evaluates the characteristics and history of a society, including a society's cultural values, and how those values are implemented in the regulation of religion. A further set of considerations flows directly from the work of Donald Black in the sociology of law, and includes important variables such as status, intimacy, and third-party partisanship, as well as evidentiary processes and production. Finally, the work of William Chambliss has identified the dialectic processes of law development as useful in allowing us to understand how legal structures protective of religious freedom might be produced.

INTRODUCTION

For the past several years I have focused on sociologically oriented efforts to explain the origins, development, and variations of concepts such as religious freedom[1] and human rights in general.[2] This work has sought to increase understanding of relationships between law, broadly defined, and religion, also broadly defined.[3] I have taken a social constructionist approach to the project, cognizant of theoretical developments in the sociology of law and the sociology of religion, cognizant also of specific historical contexts that illustrate important relationships between law and religion.

Some of my prior work treats law as both dependent upon and/or derivative from religious traditions. Other portions of the work treat law as a tool for social control and as an independent influence on religion and religious groups and organizations.[4] Still other portions of the work have examined specific instances of the way law and religion interact in various societies, either in general terms or with respect to specific religious groups. I have attended particularly to the treatment of religion and religious groups and practices by key legal institutions such as the European Court of Human Rights, and by constitutional courts, especially in countries formerly dominated by the Soviet Union.[5]

Finally, some of my earlier work dealt indirectly with legal pluralism and *Shari'a*, but did not focus specifically on these important issues. This article reports preliminary results of my foray into this area of study.

IMPORTANT VARIABLES INFLUENCING RELIGIOUS FREEDOM AND HUMAN RIGHTS

In my 2006 and 2007 articles, I have discussed a number of interrelated structural variables, processes, and historical contexts that influence the development of religious freedom and concern for human rights. One major set of variables can be grouped under the title *characteristics of legal and judicial systems*. Another set evaluates the *characteristics and history of a society*, including a society's *cultural values*, and how those values are implemented in the *regulation of religion*. A further set of considerations flows directly from the work of Donald Black[6] in the sociology of law and includes important variables such as *status*, *intimacy*, and *third party partisanship*, as well as *evidentiary processes and production*. Finally, the work of William Chambliss[7] has identified the *dialectic processes of law development* as useful in allowing us to understand how legal structures protective of religious freedom might be produced. I will briefly summarize each of these sets of variables before correlating them with the concept legal pluralism.

Characteristics of Legal and Judicial Systems

Legal and judicial systems vary greatly in terms of their *pervasiveness* and *centralization*, the *type of system (adversarial* or *inquisitorial)* they rely on, the amount of *autonomy* and *discretion* afforded the judiciary, and the *normative role* played by the judicial system in a given society.

The lives of citizens vary greatly in terms of how much a legal system impacts them personally. In societies with more pervasive legal systems, many aspects of life are influenced by formal legal considerations. In other societies, citizens can go about their daily lives without much intrusion from official legal and judicial institutions. These latter societies obviously offer much opportunity for the development of legal pluralism and informal methods of social control, as citizens of the society find ways other than formal legal proceedings to settle disputes and interact with each other.

Societies also vary in terms of how much centralized control is exerted upon their citizens. In some societies, there is one formal governmental structure, and all citizens must abide by the edicts of those who control that structure. Other societies may be much more decentralized in terms of legal authority, offering a federated approach to governing or even permitting legally pluralistic situations is develop where there are enclaves in which the centralized legal structure exercises little if any authority.

In some societies, the judicial system has considerable autonomy; judges are appointed for life or are very difficult to remove once in office. Judges in such societies usually can exercise considerable discretion, and with relative impunity. The rise of constitutional courts in many societies around the world also is a move toward a more autonomous judiciary. Further, in some regions of the world national sovereignty has been eroded when transnational judicial systems have been granted power over national legal structures. The Council of Europe (CoE) with its European Court of Human Rights (ECtHR) is by far the best known example of such a regional court system, but there are others. The interaction of the ECtHR with constitutional courts and the judicial systems of the 47 Member States of the CoE is a fascinating example of the "judicialization of politics" and the growing prominence and autonomy of judicial systems in the modern world.

In other societies, the judicial system has been granted little internal autonomy and is not subject to any external judicial system. The judiciary may be completely dominated by other institutional structures such as a political party, the military, a religious regime, or the executive or legislative branches of government. In such situations, judges may be compelled to act out the directives of others during the decision-making process for fear of losing their positions or even their lives.

All of the variables just discussed, interacting with those to be examined below, play a role in how much religious freedom and concern for human rights prevails within a given society. Unless legal and judicial systems can impact a citizen, and unless those systems can, and will, act with impunity to protect religious freedom and concern for human rights, there will be little room for the exercise of such rights.

Characteristics and History of a Society

Every society has its unique history, and that history directly impacts whether considerations about religious freedom and human rights are of concern to that society. One very important variable concerns the amount and type of *religious pluralism* present in a given society.[8] The *cultural values* of a society are crucial variable as well, as is the manner in which those values are reflected in formal documents such as *constitutions* and *statutes*. The establishment and presence of a *strong state* apparatus is important to consider, as is the manner in which a state chooses to *regulate religion* within its society. Often states choose to establish formal methods of regulating religion, including official *hierarchies* of religious groups, hierarchies that are given the force of law. Such hierarchies grant graduated privileges to religious groups depending on where they are placed on the hierarchy.

If a society is not well-differentiated in terms of religion, then there may be little concern about religious freedom. But when multiple religious traditions and groups are present in a society, the issue of religious freedom becomes salient. Indeed, how a society treats its religious minorities seems to be an ultimate test of whether that society values religious freedom. Those in control of a society may welcome multiple religious traditions and even value religious diversity; at the other extreme, a society may seek to repress and stamp out certain religious groups and expressions.

The *cultural values* of a society, as expressed in and implemented by its sacred historical governing documents, reveal much about the situation within that society regarding religious freedom. The constitutions of many modern nations include expressions of support for religious freedom, but those expressions may be honored in the breach; phrases in the governing documents may be ambiguous on some crucial issues, such as whether the religious freedom considerations enshrined in the documents refer to organizations (and if so, which ones), or whether they are focused on the religious freedom of individuals. This is a crucial point to which we will return below.

The existence of a strong state apparatus is of great import in implementing (or deterring) the religious freedom rights of citizens. If a state's political leadership chooses to implement cultural values that encourage religious freedom, those values are likely to be important within that society. But the reverse might also be the case: strong states can choose to repress religious freedom. Thus it appears that the interaction of a strong state with cultural values determines much about the level of religious freedom available to citizens and religious groups within a society.

On this point, it is useful to recount briefly the history and derivation of concern about religious freedom in human history. It appears that the Treaty of Westphalia in 1648 was the first formal legal document that contained a reference to religious freedom. This famous treaty was developed out of desperation as those in positions of power in Western Europe sought to find ways to end the religious-based wars ravaging that area. The Treaty of Westphalia gave impetus to the development of nation-states when those involved agreed that some entity other than warring religious traditions needed to be established and granted authority in order to achieve peace in that part of the world. Under the Treaty, "*third party*" states could intervene and enforce a modicum of peace by stating that vying religious traditions must learn to coexist. Religious freedom was given a tremendous boost by this political compromise and decision. The concept gained further impetus with the establishment of the United States and its carefully crafted political compromise guaranteeing religious freedom, a compromise often imitated thereafter.

Some states regulate religion by establishing *hierarchies* among religious groups, either formally through official registration mechanisms and processes or informally by using other less obvious methods.[9] In the United States, regulation is comparatively informal, left to governmental agencies such as the Internal Revenue Service (IRS). The IRS has developed a long list of criteria it applies when a group requests tax-exempt status. In many other nations, some sort of official "ministry of religion" vets applications for official recognition of religious entities and places groups according to criteria developed within that nation. Such hierarchies are often multilevel and include officially sanctioned religious organizations, one of which may have or acquire special status as the official religion of the nation. Further down the hierarchy are tolerated groups with some legal privileges and the right to function openly. Toward the bottom of such hierarchies are groups not tolerated and/or not allowed to operate openly, groups that have few or no legal privileges. Obviously the existence of a hierarchy among religions within a society has immense implications for the religious freedom of the society's citizenry. And the very presence of groups not officially tolerated raises the ironic possibility that such groups, when forced underground, may develop their own methods of social control, in effect creating a form of legal pluralism.

Sociology of Law Variables and Processes

Black[10] has proposed that variables such a *social status and prestige* and *personal and cultural intimacy* play crucial roles in determining who prevails when matters are dealt with by legal and judicial systems. Black and Baumgartner[11] also have developed the concept *third party partisan* to analyze how judicial systems function and how those low in status and intimacy can sometimes prevail in legal battles. Chambliss and Zatz[12] proposes a continual *dialectic process model* to explain how major legal developments occur and how temporary legal and political *resolutions* are developed to respond to the *contractions* and *conflicts* that can arise within a society, given the immense differences in power and access to resources that exist in most societies. Also germane to how legal systems operate are *rules of evidence* and decisions made about what evidence is to be *produced* and *admitted* in legal proceedings.

The theories of Black and of Chambliss, taken together, offer much to our understanding of the development of legal systems, how they function, and which entities usually prevail when legal systems are used to settle disputes or enact social control. Chambliss is primarily interested in what he terms "points at which laws are produced that provide a new approach to a problem" and cases that "strike out in a new direction" and "constitute important turning points in the historical process."[13] Certainly the development of ideas about religious freedom exemplify such major turning points in jurisprudential history. Instances where religious freedom for specific minority groups and individuals is legally established and enforced might also qualify as significant turning points.

Black is primarily focused on "who wins and why?" when legal systems are used to settle disputes or exert social control over individuals and groups. He notes that persons with high status and prestige not only usually prevail within the legal system of the society in which they reside, but even help to develop the legal system itself in ways that serve their interests. Black emphasizes that those using the legal system have more success when they share cultural values and personal characteristics, if not personal intimacy, with decision makers in the system. And when a party prevails unexpectedly, Black (with Baumgartner)[14] suggests that some "third party partisans" who do share important characteristics with decision makers have often entered the fray on behalf of the unexpected winner. This latter concept may be very useful in helping us to understand situations where minority religious groups prevail in disputes, fending off efforts by others to exert control over them.

One important aspect of how judicial systems operate concerns what counts as evidence in a legal action. Also, issues of who has standing to present evidence to the court arise; societies vary greatly about acceptable rules of procedure in this regard. Mark Cooney,[15] a student of Black, has demonstrated that the production of evidence is a social process, subject to understandable influences that will usually determine who prevails in a legal action. Richardson[16] has examined the large amount of discretion concerning evidence production and acceptance granted in cases involving minority religious groups, citing especially two famous cases from Australia (the "dingo case" involving Lindy Chamberlain and the "Hilton bombing" case involving the Ananda Marga group), as well as "brainwashing" cases from the United States and elsewhere.

A focus on evidentiary rules reveals that when unpopular religious groups are involved in legal actions, decision makers (judges) may allow in otherwise weak or unacceptable evidence *or* fail to force the production of, and allow admission of, exculpatory evidence. Such evidentiary decisions often determine the outcome of the legal action. Clearly analysis of how legal systems operate is of great moment as we try to understand the level of religious freedom available in a society. The failure of the justice system to grant a modicum of freedom and fairness to minority faiths and their members encourages the development of other, more informal methods of social control. Thus it should be noted again that an ironic outcome of a lack of perceived fairness in the treatment of minority religious groups encourages the development of legal pluralism, a topic to which we now turn.

LEGAL PLURALISM

Legal pluralism is a complex and multifaceted concept, addressed by a large scholarly literature from multiple fields. Treatments of the topic abound in law reviews and academic journals from anthropology, political science, sociology, and socio-legal studies. Sally Merry's much-cited *Law and Society Review* article (1988) claims, "Legal pluralism is a central theme in the reconceptualization of the law/society relation."[17] Merry breaks the field of legal pluralism into two major periods, the "classical period" that deals with efforts to impose the legal systems of colonial powers on colonized societies and the "new legal pluralism," which understands that all modern societies sustain varying degrees and types of legal pluralism.

In a thoroughgoing critical analysis, Brian Tamanaha[18] spends considerable time systematically describing legal pluralisms extant in the medieval period in Western Europe, reminding us that the social conditions often defined as illustrating legal pluralism occurred long before the colonial period. Tamanaha goes on to evaluate legal pluralism in the colonial period and in the globalized world of the late twentieth century, critiquing ways in which the concept has developed and suggesting how best to proceed with future theoretical development concerning legal pluralism.

Paul Berman, in a *University of Southern California Law Review* article (2007), proposes the concept "hybrid legal spaces"[19] to describe what happens in a "world of multiple normative communities." Berman points out that, according to his count, some 125 international institutions exercise some legal authority over individual nations or subsets of nations,[20] not to mention the many agreements between nations that govern activities among and between agreeing partners. Signatories of these kinds of agreements are bound by them to some degree. Berman contrasts "pure" sovereigntist and universalist approaches, demonstrating that neither work well in today's complex and globalized world, thus requiring the acceptance, even desirability, of "hybridity." *Hybridity* is a condition of provisional compromises about how to proceed with commerce and other forms of social intercourse.[21] Berman goes on to present a series of "procedural mechanisms, institutional designs, and discursive practices for managing hybridity"[22]:

1. Dialectic Legal Interactions
2. Margins of Appreciation
3. Limited Autonomy Regimes
4. Subsidiarity Schemes
5. Jurisdictional Redundancies
6. Hybrid Participation Arrangements

7. Mutual Recognition Regimes
8. Safe Harbor Agreements
9. A Pluralist Approach to Conflict of Laws

More directly to the point of this article, the International Council on Human Rights published a report of its "Research Project on Plural Legal Orders and Human Rights" in 2008.[23] The ICHR report examines various aspects of plural legal orders and the role of Non-State Legal Orders (NSLO) in working with states to promote protections for human rights. One part of the report presents a nonexhaustive list of eight ways states "enable" plural legal orders:

1. The state may choose to . . . recognize or even create institutions and authorities outside of the formal legal system to mediate and settle disputes.
2. The state may apply different laws, especially those that affect personal status . . . to different people depending on their religious identity. . . . Similarly, in many states indigenous people are subject, to varying degrees, to their own customary legal orders. . . .
3. The state may apply different personal status law regimes but may provide for a common civil law (such as a civil law of marriage) that will allow people to *cross-over*. . . .
4. The state may completely exempt certain legal orders from its remit such as provisions . . . that exempt customary law from conformity with Constitutional standards.
5. The state may recognize the special status of customary legal orders but only in so far as they are not contrary to Constitutional standards. . . .
6. The state may exempt certain geographical areas from its formal legal regime and recognize normative orders prevailing therein as law. . . . In . . . these regions there are some Constitutional exceptions with respect to indigenous legal orders.
7. Situations of conflict, or transition from conflict, also create situations within states for the creation of plural legal orders, such as in occupied territories. . . .
8. In addition, the predatory, discriminatory, weak, ineffective, and/or inaccessible nature of the state's legal institutions, or indeed their "inappropriate" form or substance may lead to the further strengthening and growth of a range of *local* legal orders. These may be entirely endogenous or indeed

hybrid versions/improvisations of traditional mechanisms that communities, especially the poor and vulnerable, rely on to settle disputes and conflicts.

A SOCIOLOGICAL APPROACH TO LEGAL PLURALISM

The analyses of legal pluralism briefly discussed above are but a few of the efforts to develop the concept in an analytically useful manner. These studies offer useful descriptions and categorizations of what is to be found around the globe in terms of examples of legal pluralism and how such legally pluralistic situations operate. However, to date I have not found what I would call a straightforward, systematic, sociological examination of legal pluralism that attempts to explain why it occurs, when it occurs, and what variables affect the form it might take in a specific social and historical context. Further, I have found some discussions of the relationship of legal pluralism to concepts such as religious freedom or human rights. Treatments covering this latter issue have focused on the potential conflict between allowing religiously based normative systems to have the force of law when doing so may limit the personal freedom of individuals within a group, particularly women. While a very important issue, this singular concern should not constrain a more thorough examination of the relationship between religious freedom and legal pluralism.

What follows is an effort to apply certain concepts and ideas used in my earlier efforts to explain the sociological and historical circumstances that foster religious freedom and human rights in general[24] to the context of legal pluralism. Another way to state my approach is that I want to treat legal pluralism as something of a *mediating variable* between the structural and socio-legal concepts I have used previously as independent variables, and the dependent variable of religious freedom. Hopefully this effort will provoke additional research and shed light on the complicated ways in which religious freedom may be fostered (or hindered) in today's legally pluralistic world.

Before beginning this effort I must return to the issue raised earlier about the distinction between religious freedom for individuals and religious freedom for groups or organizations. Sometimes these two foci of religious freedom clash, and some examples of legal pluralism clearly demonstrate this possibility. If a religious group is allowed to exercise the full range of its norms and values in an informal legal system sanctioned (or ignored) by the State in which it resides, doing so may interfere with the rights of individual members of the group who might prefer *not* to be bound by those norms and values. As noted, this issue has been raised with respect to the role of women in some religious traditions,[25] but it can impinge on other aspects of individual religious freedom as well, such as the prerogative to change religious affiliations.

Thus, this important distinction between forms of religious freedom should be taken into account as we proceed to discuss the impact of selected variables on legal pluralism and hence on religious freedom for those affected when legal pluralistic solutions are allowed within a society.

Characteristics of Legal and Judicial Systems

If a legal system is *pervasive* and affects the lives of most citizens of a society, it in all likelihood operates to limit legal pluralism within the society. It is theoretically possible, of course, for a pervasive legal system to be applied differentially, allowing a sociologically defined enclave to operate somewhat differently from the dominant society. Indeed, some theorists (such as Donald Black) expect different applications of law depending on where a person is located in social space. However, generally we would expect an inverse relationship to exist between the *pervasiveness of a legal system* and *the presence of legal pluralism* within a society.

Similar comments can be made about the *centralization of legal systems*. The more centralized the legal system, the less we would expect to see legal pluralism flourish. In fact the amount of legal pluralism that exists in a society is an empirical question, as shown by the report of the International Council on Human Rights (2008),[26] which noted many different arrangements allowing some form of legal pluralism. Leaders of a society with a highly centralized legal system can potentially decide to allow legally pluralistic enclaves and enforce such accommodating edicts by virtue of its centralized control.

Judicial systems vary greatly in terms of autonomy, discretion, and impunity of action. Such variations can affect the degree of religious freedom within a given society as well as the development of legal pluralism. It seems a truism to state that unless a judiciary can protect itself, it cannot protect the religious freedom of politically weaker and unpopular religious groups and their members. However, even if judges are protected and the judiciary in a country has considerable autonomy and discretion, the values implemented in decisions by the judiciary can work either for or against religious freedom, for or against the development of legal pluralism. In some cases, the constitution or the statutes of a nation protect minority faiths, allowing them to operate in legally pluralistic ways. Under such circumstances, judges can allow religious groups to act independently to some extent even if those groups are unpopular with most members of the dominant society. If legal pluralism is defined by the dominant society, it can be enforced by the judicial system of the society. Thus if legal pluralism is sanctioned by the State and the governing documents of the dominant society, and if the judiciary is adequately protected as it makes decisions, then legal pluralism can be enforced for use by minority groups.

Characteristics and History of a Society

Clearly, the more *religiously pluralistic* a society, the more likely we are to find legal pluralism. The greater the number of religious groups that operate within a certain geographic area, the more likely some of them are to seek to develop informal rules about how to deal with certain issues among the membership. Family matters (divorce, custody, inheritance, division of property, etc.) are particularly targeted by minority faiths as they attempt to govern or at least influence the lives of their members. Political leaders of the dominant society may decide to expend resources to enforce societal norms, but they may also decide that it is more efficient and less trouble to allow informal systems to develop. Indeed, some societies may even officially sanction *legal enclaves*, or turn a blind eye to them, allowing groups to function as they choose within the confines of the dominant society; some overarching restrictions may apply.

A society with a *strong state apparatus* may seek to impose its legal system and values on all citizens. However, when this is done an enormous outlay of resources may be required to maintain such a rigid social order. Political leaders may eventually decide that costs in terms of resources (and negative international publicity) are not worth the effort. Of course, the values of the society's political leaders can also be implemented to allow more flexibility, thus protecting some forms of legal pluralism and the attendant religious freedoms of members allowed such flexibility. We could empirically test whether the more usual case involving a strong state would see significant pressures toward uniformity, with less legal pluralism allowed. We can also empirically test other characteristics of a society that might play a major role in determining whether legal pluralism and religious freedom might be allowed. For instance, if a strong state also has an autonomous judiciary that can critique the actions of the executive and legislative branches of government with impunity, more legal pluralism (and religious freedom) might exist for unpopular religious minorities than would otherwise be the case.

As indicated above, many societies develop formal or informal *hierarchies among religious groups and traditions*, which allow selected groups to receive benefits denied to other groups, such as access to schools, the media, the military, tax revenues, and other forms of assistance. Religious groups ranked lower in the hierarchy would have fewer benefits; some at the very bottom would have none and perhaps even operate at their peril within the society. It seems commonsensical that the higher a religious group ranks in whatever hierarchy exists, the more likely it would be allowed to develop its own internal set of normative and even legally binding structures. A corollary to this prediction might be that the amount of legal autonomy afforded a minority religious group would also depend on the amount of resources and effort the dominant society has to expend to force a minority group to abide by the norms and rules of the dominant society. In short, sometimes those in charge of institutions of social control in a society might decide it is too much trouble to enforce all the rules of the society within a given enclave. Under such circumstances political leaders of the dominant class might decide to leave minority religious groups to their own devices, thus allowing informal legal pluralism to develop.

I have earlier predicted that the presence of an adversarial-based legal system would increase the chances of successfully defending religious freedom. It seems logical to assume that the presence of an adversarial system could also promote legal pluralism. If a minority religious group can obtain the services of strong and experienced legal assistance in battles with authorities, it will have a better chance to defend itself as it attempts to develop a form of legal pluralism to serve the group's interest. Hiring legal counsel within an adversarial legal system can be thought of a one form of "*third party partisanship*" (see discussion below). In an inquisitorial system, those in charge of the judicial system determine who (if anyone) will offer testimony or other support for those charged with violating laws or those who seek redress in civil legal actions. Such a situation would usually seem to preclude the involvement of a significant *third party partisan* on behalf of a minority religious group or person, thus limiting the chances for successful development of legal pluralism.

Sociology of Law Variables and Processes

Minority religious groups by definition have less *status and prestige* than other religious groups. This lack of social standing adheres to most group members as well. Also by definition, in many minority faiths members and leaders share little *personal or cultural intimacy* with members of the dominant classes. They live in separate worlds governed by different sets of norms and values.

Given such separateness, the achievement of any degree of legal autonomy by a minority religious group seems problematic. When legal autonomy occurs, explanation is needed. Official policies sanctioning multiculturalism enforced by officials within a dominant society can contribute to the development of enclaves of legal pluralism. But why such policies develop is itself a question of import. Policies sanctioning multiculturalism could result from enlightened leadership within the dominant class, coupled with a "squeaking wheel gets the grease" attitude brought on by the persistent efforts of a minority faith to implement its norms and values in certain areas of life. Enlightened leadership and the persistence of the minority group both could be related to the presence of values that allow and encourage pluralism within that society. Alternatively, officials governing the society could simply decide that it is less trouble to allow the development of legally pluralistic enclaves for certain minority religious groups.

How religious groups implement any granted flexibility associated with legal pluralism should be analyzed carefully. Some groups may limit personal freedoms as they develop legal pluralism for the collective. Leaders of the dominant class may choose to ignore breaches of dominant societal values in the interest of maintaining a semblance of control over minority religious groups, as well as peace in the streets.

One important variable to consider when legal pluralism is allowed to exist concerns the possible presence of *third party partisans* mentioned previously. If minority religions lack social status and personal or cultural intimacy with decision makers in the society, they may nonetheless sometimes attract support from persons who have some of those characteristics or who have the authority to enforce values different from those held by decision makers in the dominant society. This "*strange attractor*" phenomenon needs more research, but it is clear that sometimes strange attractions may occur and assist minority religious groups in developing additional religious freedom and autonomy. This could contribute to the development of legal pluralism.

Analysis of how, why, and when third party partisans are attracted to minority groups would also help us to understand how specific *dialectic processes* that develop in modern societies can lead to conflicts if not resolved. One possible resolution to potential conflicts between minority religious groups and the dominant society would be to allow legal pluralism to develop. We need to explain how and why formal sanctioning of legal pluralism occurs. And even if no formal legal approval for legal pluralism occurs but religious groups are allowed to go their own way to some extent anyway, we should analyze and define the process of negotiation and compromise that takes place. Arguably formal or informal legal pluralistic situations would not develop for minority religious groups unless parties with status and prestige intervened on behalf of the group. How, when and why this occurs are empirical questions that need to be addressed.

EXCURSUS ON *SHARI'A*

Given the theme of this issue, an obvious question might arise as to how the theorizing and hypothesizing suggested above relates to the spread of *Shari'a* in societies where Muslim minorities have developed. I contend that the variables briefly discussed in this section not only help us to explain the development (or not) of legal pluralism, they also potentially help us to explain specifically how *Shari'a* systems might develop and be allowed to flourish within certain societies.

In religiously pluralistic societies with less pervasive legal systems, the presence of a persistent minority such as Islam should find it easier to gain acceptance, even reluctantly, for its type of legal pluralism. In a more centralized legal system, the very fact of centralization, especially in a "strong State," could work in favor of a *Shari'a* based legal pluralism, so long as societal authorities become convinced that the easiest way to deal with a Muslim minority would be to allow it its own legal enclave to settle certain personal matters. Where the legal system is adversarial in nature, legal enclaves might be accomplished more easily if the Muslim group retains a socially well-placed "third party partisan" to carry its legal battles or if prominent individuals or groups within the dominant society decide to assist in establishing a legal pluralistic enclave for the minority group.

If a society's sacred legal documents allow or even encourage the establishment of legal pluralistic enclaves, those documents would assist Muslim groups in founding legal enclaves. If the judiciary is relatively autonomous, and judges share pluralistic values, then they might be more prone to allow legal pluralism to operate in Muslim communities, even in the face of opposition. Decisions to permit the operation of *Shari'a* could be even more likely if some members of the Muslim community achieve high social status and prestige and if they share cultural and personal values with those in decision-making positions within the dominant society. Alternatively, if socially well-placed third parties can be found to defend and speak on behalf of the Muslim community, then this could also have a positive influence on those making decisions about the acceptance of legal pluralism for Muslim communities.

All of these variables working together can help us to understand the dialectic processes undertaken as a society attempts to deal with contradictions and conflicts that can arise when a Muslim community emerges within a culture with quite different norms and values. As resolutions are sought to potential conflicts between Muslim and non-Muslim groups, dialectically achieved resolutions should be explicable in terms of the operation of variables outlined above.

One caution is in order, however, when we differentiate the religious freedom of groups from the religious freedom of individuals. This distinction may also help us to explain the specific character of any legally pluralistic resolution involving *Shari'a*. Efforts to promote *Shari'a* may generate opposition from those who value individual religious freedom and other individual civil and human rights, especially for women, and may also generate opposition from those who value the right to change religions, among other concerns.[27] Such interests, both internal and external to Muslim groups, will undoubtedly play a role in dialectic processes that have the capacity to produce legal pluralism and will condition resolutions adopted at any given time.

NOTES

1. James T. Richardson, "Religion, Constitutional Courts, and Democracy in Former Communist Countries," *The Annals of the American Academy of Political and Social*

Science 603 (2006): 129–38; James T. Richardson, "The Sociology of Religious Freedom: A Structural and Socio-Legal Analysis," *Sociology of Religion* 67 (2006): 271–29.

2. James T. Richardson, "Religion, Law, and Human Rights," in *Religion, Globalization, and Culture*, ed. Peter Beyer and Lori Beaman (London: Brill, 2007), 407–28; James T. Richardson, "Protection of Religious Minorities in States with Dominant Religions: The Role of the Courts," in *Quo Vadis Eastern Europe? Religion, State, and Society after Communism*, ed. Ines Murzaku (Bologna: University of Bologna Press, 2007), 107–121.

3. For one example, see James T. Richardson, ed., *Regulating Religion: Case Studies from Around the Globe* (New York: Kluwer, 2004).

4. James T. Richardson, "Religion and Law: An Interactionist Perspective," in *The Oxford Handbook of the Sociology of Religion*, ed. Peter Clarke (Oxford: Oxford University Press, 2009), 418–31; James T. Richardson, "Scientology in Court: A Look at Some Major Cases from Various Nations," in *Scientology*, ed. James Lewis (Oxford: Oxford University Press, 2009), 283–94; James Beckford and James T. Richardson, "Regulating Religion," in *Handbook for the Sociology of Religion*, ed. J. Beckford and J. Demerath (London: Routledge, 2007), 396–418.

5. James T. Richardson and Alain Garay, "The European Court of Human Rights and Former Communist States" in *Religion and Patterns of Social Transformation*, ed. D. M. Jerolimov, S. Zrinscak, and I. Borowik (Zagreb: Institute for Social Research, 2004), 223–34; James T. Richardson and Jennifer Shoemaker, "The European Court of Human Rights, Minority Religions, and the Social Construction of Religious Freedom," in *The Centrality of Religion in Social Life*, ed. Eileen Barker (Aldershot: Ashgate, 2008), 103–16; Richardson, "Religion, Constitutional Courts, and Democracy."

6. Donald Black, *The Social Structure of Right and Wrong* (New York: Academic Press, 1999).

7. William Chambliss and Marjorie Zatz, *Making Law: The State, the Law, and Structural Contradictions* (Bloomington, University of Indiana Press, 1993).

8. For a thorough discussion of this variable, see James Beckford, *Social Theory and Religion* (Cambridge: Cambridge University Press, 2003).

9. James T. Richardson, "Law, Social Control, and Minority Religions," in *Frontier Religions in Public Space*, ed. P. Cote (Ottawa: University of Ottawa Press, 2001), 139–68; James T. Richardson, "'Showtime in Texas': A Sociological Analysis of the Branch Davidian Trials," *Nova Religio* 5 (2001): 152–70.

10. Black, *The Social Structure of Right and Wrong*.

11. Donald Black and M. Baumgartner, "Toward a Theory of the Third Party," in *The Social Structure of Right and Wrong*, ed. D. Black (New York: Academic Press, 1999), 95–124.

12. Chambliss and Zatz, *Making Law*.

13. Ibid., 5–6.

14. Black and Baumgartner, "Toward a Theory of the Third Party."

15. Mark Cooney, "Evidence as Partisanship," *Law and Society Review* 28 (1994): 833–58.

16. James T. Richardson, "Discretion and Discrimination in Legal Cases Involving Controversial Religious Groups and Allegations of Ritual Abuse," in *Law and Religion*, ed. Rex Ahdar (Aldershot: Ashgate, 2000), 11–132

17. Sally E. Merry, "Legal Pluralism," *Law and Society Review* 22 (1988): 869.

18. Brian Tamanaha, "Understanding Legal Pluralism: Past, to Present, Local to Global," *University of Sydney Law Review* 30 (2009): 375–411.

19. Paul S. Berman, "Global Legal Pluralism," *University of Southern California Law Review* 80 (2007): 1157–158.

20. Ibid., 1160.

21. Ibid., 1165.

22. Ibid., 1196–234.

23. International Council on Human Rights Policy, "Research Project on Plural Legal Orders and Human Rights: An Approach Paper" (Geneva: ICHRP, June 2008).

24. Richardson, "Law, Social Control, and Minority Religions"; Richardson, "The Sociology of Religious Freedom"; Richardson, "Religion, Law, and Human Rights."

25. Linda McClain, "Marriage Pluralism in the United States: On Civil and Religious Jurisdiction and the Demands of Equal Citizenship" (Boston University School of Law Working Paper No. 10–14, May 24, 2010).

26. International Council on Human Rights Policy, "Research Project."

27. McClain, "Marriage Pluralism in the United States."

Index

Note:
Page numbers in **bold** type refer to figures
Page numbers in *italic* type refer to tables
Page numbers followed by 'n' refer to notes

For Product Safety Concerns and Information please contact our
EU representative GPSR@taylorandfrancis.com Taylor & Francis
Verlag GmbH, Kaufingerstraße 24, 80331 München, Germany